# POINTERS
# TO ETERNITY

# POINTERS TO ETERNITY

## Dewi Rees MD FRCGP BS

*For Valerie*

First impression: 2010

© Dewi Rees and Y Lolfa 2010

ISBN: 9781847711991

Printed on acid-free and partly recycled paper
and published and bound in Wales by
Y Lolfa Cyf., Talybont, Ceredigion SY24 5HE
*e-mail* ylolfa@ylolfa.com
*website* www.ylolfa.com
*tel* 01970 832 304
*fax* 832 782

# CONTENTS

# Introduction

BELIEF IN LIFE AFTER death is a central tenet of all religions. The nature of this afterlife is not clear, and the form it takes is not well defined, but the belief is universal and rooted in human history. There are cultural and geographical variations – for instance the Eastern idea of reincarnation differs from the traditional beliefs of tribal Africa and of China – yet each asserts a continued existence for the deceased. Differences also exist in the doctrines of the main monotheistic religions (Islam, Judaism and Christianity), but a belief in the afterlife and the Resurrection of the dead is central to each. This certainty of belief has its critics, notably Professor Richard Dawkins in our present day and Epicurus in ancient Greece, who say that there is no objective evidence to support a belief in life after death. This is true, but the available evidence does point to the reality of an afterlife. The evidence is subjective, but it has its own reality and is deeply engrained in the experiences and psyches of people everywhere. More specifically, studies on bereavement provide support for this traditional view.

The purpose of this book is to consider three types of evidence from my perspective as a medical doctor. First, I present the opinions of 67 retired Anglican bishops on the Resurrection, together with their own accounts (where applicable) of experiencing the presence of Jesus. The bishops provided this information in response to a letter and questionnaire which I sent them. (The reply rate was over 80 per cent.) The second approach provides accounts of other recent meetings with Jesus, including instances where the percipients were convinced that they had seen Jesus in his human form. Most of these encounters have not been reported before, though some have had a limited circulation elsewhere. Thirdly, the book reviews recent research on people's experiences of their dead spouses, and considers its relevance to an understanding of the universal belief in the afterlife and to Christian teaching on the Resurrection.

The book has twelve chapters arranged in four sections: Beginnings, Bishops, Visions and the Widowed. The first chapter is my personal foreword which explains my background and personal beliefs, and sets the scene for the more substantial sections later. Chapter 2 provides a brief review of Jesus' life and death and considers the question: 'Why did Jesus die so quickly on the cross?'. It also discusses the belief held by Muslims that Jesus did not die on the cross. Chapter 3 looks at the disciples' experiences of the Resurrection, including their grief and fears for their own safety. Chapters 4 and 5 deal with the bishops' responses to my letter and questionnaire. The four following chapters contain accounts of recent encounters with Jesus, with Chapter 8 focussing on deathbed experiences and Chapter 9 on appearances to people of non-Christian faiths. The two penultimate chapters ask how much significance should be ascribed to widowed peoples' experiences of their dead spouses when assessing the Resurrection and the reality of the afterlife. The final chapter draws conclusions.

Many people have helped in the writing of the book and I am grateful to them all, especially those whose letters and comments are to be found within its pages. My special thanks go to Professors John Copas and John Roberts, my daughters Anna Asquith and Eileen Rees, and my nephew Peter Cooke.

Finally, I wish to say that the book has a theme but is not a narrative. Consequently, readers may be selective in deciding the order in which the sections are read, as each tends to be an entity in itself.

# Section 1

# Beginnings

CHAPTER 1

# Personal Foreword

B OOKS ON THE RESURRECTION are usually written by theologians who are senior members of the Christian, Islamic or Jewish faiths. This book is different: I am a medical man looking at the Resurrection and expectations of an afterlife with a scientific approach, using data which I have, in the main, collected myself. As I have no religious status and do not usually consider questions of faith, readers may wonder from what background and with what authority I approach such an important topic. Hence this personal foreword.

I am an 80-year-old retired family physician and hospice doctor who is nearing the end of his life's journey. I was born in South Wales in 1929, when memories of the Welsh Revival of 1904 were still alive. Although short-lived, that resurgence of faith had a big impact outside Wales with repercussions in Africa, India, the USA and elsewhere. [1] It preceded, and was probably a catalyst for, the Pentecostal fervour that erupted from the Azusa Street Methodist Chapel in Los Angeles in 1906, which spread rapidly to many parts of the States. [2] George Jeffreys, founder of the Elim Pentecostal Movement, received the gift of the Holy Spirit during the Revival, and three Bible schools were founded in Wales which trained missionaries to work at home and abroad. [3,4] One school, the South Wales Bible College, was established close to my home and I had a passing acquaintance with its principal and some of the students.

My parents were both Welsh Baptists. My father joined my

mother in the denomination when he was wooing her. (He was brought up in the Anglican tradition.) They knew of the Revival and my father would have attended meetings, but he was not closely involved with it. On Sunday evenings he used to take me to a small mission church known locally as the 'Navvy Mission', so named because it was built for the itinerant workmen, called 'navigators', who built the docks at Barry – the town in which I was born. The sermons preached at the mission tended towards the 'hell fire and brimstone' variety, the preachers often being visiting evangelists or young men training for the ministry. The hymns were by Sankey and Moody and were sung with enormous gusto. The Rev Dr Paisley, the well-known Northern Ireland cleric and politician, may have preached there, having been enrolled as a student at the South Wales Bible College when only 16 by his father, who was a close friend of the principal, Mr BS Fidler. In later years, Dr Paisley would say that he had got his theology from Ulster but had learned to preach in Barry. He probably gained this early skill because it was then normal practice for the college students to hold open-air missions on the sands of Barry Island and to preach in the square in front of the town hall while standing on a box. Br Ramon was another well-known alumnus of the Bible College. He became an Anglican priest, head of the Franciscan community at Glasshampton, and a prolific writer of books in the style of Thomas Merton.

As a boy, I went with my mother to a Welsh Baptist chapel called Calfaria, where we always sat in the back pew. Being a Welsh congregation in an English-speaking town the numbers were small, and even in those days – the mid 1930s to early 1940s – the place was almost empty. I understood little of what was said; a drawback that I regard as advantageous with hindsight, because it enabled me to be more aware of the spiritual atmosphere and of the sense of wonder and worship that is at the heart of religion. On communion Sundays, which were solemn and important occasions, I shared with my mother the sacraments that the deacons brought to her in a tiny glass and paten. I liked the Welsh hymns and would sing them wholeheartedly, without knowing what the words meant. These hymns were particularly moving at the family funerals which I attended with my mother as 'the male representative' of the family, and though everything was in Welsh, I was deeply moved by the atmosphere, the sense of grief and the family unity I perceived.

## Bereavements

Mother died at the age of 65 and I was present at her death. (Because of its personal significance, this event is dealt with in detail in the chapter on deathbed experiences.) She was a quiet, unassuming lady whom I now regard as one of the more spiritually evolved women I have known. I base this assessment to a large extent on the way she handled the last 18 months of her life, when she was terminally ill with cancer. She was not a gregarious person and when Calfaria closed as a Welsh centre of worship, she ceased to be a church or chapel goer. In retirement she had few other links within the community, but she nurtured herself with the Bible and Bunyan's *Pilgrims Progress*. When, because of her illness, my parents came to live with us, I introduced her to some of the great spiritual classics of Christianity, including *The Cloud of Unknowing;* Julian of Norwich's *Revelation of Divine Love; The Way of a Pilgrim;* Thomas Kelly's *A Testament of Devotion;* and to inspirational works from other religions like the *Bhagavad-Gita*. She absorbed these books avidly and it was quite amazing to see how her spirit seemed to enlarge as her body faded and to watch her get out of her sickbed to help my father in the last few days of his life. Father died six weeks before Mother, seemingly of grief. He was 14 years older than her and they had left their own home to live in a strange house and town so that she could be cared for by my wife and myself. He died in 1964, on the same day that I delivered a baby by forceps. This was an unusual procedure for a general practitioner to undertake, but it was necessary and it was good to know that I had helped to bring a new life into this world as my father's life reached its end.

I was amazed by the depth of grief that I experienced when my mother died. I had always felt closer to my father but it was her death that hurt the most. I had imagined I would be immune to such a response, having gone to a boarding school, Llandovery College, at the age of 12, and then, like most young men, being conscripted into the army in my late teens. After completing my army service, I went to medical school in London, got married and started my own family. I had seen many deaths and did not expect to be very distressed when my parents died, or to feel the pain of bereavement so intensely or for so long afterwards. But having experienced the pain of bereavement, I became more interested in the way it affected other people and wished to know about their reactions to such a loss. One consequence was that I published two early papers on bereavement. The first was written in conjunction with the statistician Sylvia Lutkins; it was entitled *The Mortality of Bereavement* [5] and was published in the *British Medical Journal* in 1967. The second paper was based on my MD thesis and was entitled *The Hallucinations of Widowhood* [6]; it was also published in the *British Medical Journal*. The results are relevant to this book and will be discussed in Chapters 10 and 11.

My papers on bereavement were published in 1967 and 1971. At this time I also became increasingly interested in the care of dying patients, and although I never planned to leave general practice, it was perhaps inevitable that I would specialize in palliative medicine and move into the then new and rapidly-developing field of hospice care. I did this in a somewhat circuitous way but hospice work did enable me to combine two of my major interests: the care of the dying and bereaved, and comparative religion. Eventually, I was appointed Medical Director of St Mary's Hospice in Birmingham, a Catholic foundation with an ecumenical and interfaith policy in its attitude to patients. This inclusive approach was recognized by the ethnic communities in the city and they allowed us to become closely involved in the care of their members, both at home and in the unit. Our patients included Hindus, Jews, Sikhs and Muslims, and some invited us to attend their mourning ceremonies. This was a great privilege and it enabled members of the staff, particularly those working on the Home Care Team, to gain a greater insight into the beliefs and practices of other cultures.

## Attitudes and experiences

Church attendance has declined greatly in the United Kingdom in recent decades, despite the best efforts of church leaders to reverse this trend. Many people who are still Christian at heart no longer feel a need to attend church on a regular basis, but I am not one of those individuals. I am always prepared to discuss and explain my position to anyone who wishes to know it, but I have no wish to proselytise and convert others to my beliefs and I think it would be wrong for me to do so. I do hold to the Christian faith, and whilst my practical involvement diminishes I remain a regular worshipper at Coventry Cathedral and nearby churches. In the past I have held many of the appointments open to lay members of the Anglican communion. These included membership of the Diocesan Synods of Bangor and Coventry, and membership of the Governing Body of the Church in Wales. More recently I was a guide at Coventry Cathedral. I have worked closely with clergy of many denominations and number some as friends. These contacts were facilitated by the nature and range of my professional work, which was mainly as a general practitioner in England, Labrador, and rural Wales, and later as medical director of St Mary's Hospice in Birmingham. Other roles included working as the medical officer at a Catholic boarding school, as a senior civil servant, and as a bereavement counsellor at a prison for young offenders. I am naturally ecumenical and am interested in people's inner experiences and their awareness of the numinous – the sense of mystery and awe that people experience at the presence of the divine.

## Contacting the bishops

My involvement with the Church and interest in bereavement had an unexpected outcome. I began to realize that the experiences of many widowed people and the events associated with the Resurrection were not totally dissimilar and that a useful relationships might exist between them. Seeking further information, I wrote to people who I hoped might help to elucidate some of my uncertainties. In the first instance I wrote to a group of Christians called Cursillistas, resident in the Diocese of Coventry,. These, I knew, were firm in their faith and likely to reply to my letter. I also wrote to most of the retired Anglican bishops living in England. The results were impressive.

Some people have asked why I chose these two groups rather than members of the medical profession. I chose the bishops because they could be expected to speak on the subject with an authority and range of experience that others might lack. The Cursillistas, who are mainly lay people, were chosen because they have a natural interest in the subject and would be more likely to reply to my letters than agnostics or people of other faiths. I excluded the medical profession mainly for the reason mentioned by Sir Thomas Browne (1605–1682) in his book *Religio Medici* (A Doctor's Religion) where, speaking of the medical profession's reputation for disbelief, he quoted an aphorism current at the time, that when three physicians met together you would find two atheists. Sir Thomas' assessment agreed with my own experience of medical doctors, although these days they are more are likely to be agnostics than atheists. To be fair, however, this view does not tally with a study made in 1996 at a meeting of the American Academy of Family Physicians, where 99% of the physicians surveyed were convinced that religious beliefs can heal, and 75% believed that prayers of others can promote a patient's recovery. [7]

In July 2004, I sent a three-point questionnaire to 82 retired Anglican bishops (see Appendix 3). I asked them to complete the questionnaire and to let me know their views on the Resurrection and, if possible, of any personal experiences they may have had of the risen Jesus that might be similar to those recorded in the Gospels. The response rate was high (over 81%) and the generous way the bishops provided detailed information was exceptional. I have had no such mystical experiences, but in asking people to read this book it is incumbent upon me to report any unusual personal incidents that may be relevant to the readership. I have had no visions and, although widowed, I have not sensed the presence of my dear wife. (Almost half of widowed people have reportedly experienced their partner's presence.) Similarly, I have had no out-of-the-body or near-death experiences. However, there have been moments when I have been intuitively aware of the crises affecting others. Only some of these occasions are relevant to this book, but one that is imprinted in my memory involved my wife Valerie and my daughter Anna. It took place when Anna was about two years old, when we were living in mid Wales in a house that stood on a hillside overlooking the river Clywedog. I was walking near the riverbank one afternoon, when I became certain that one of my female relatives was in trouble. For no reason in particular, I thought it was probably my mother and that she was seriously ill. I turned around immediately and went back to the house, to find Anna lying deeply unconscious in Valerie's arms. She had been standing on a desk by an open window and had fallen out of the window onto a concrete path some three or four feet below. When I realized what had happened I was deeply disturbed and wondered how best to deal with the situation – whether to phone my partner, a very experienced doctor who was masterful in emergencies, or to arrange her immediate admission to the hospital some 30 miles away. Instead, I picked Anna up gently and to my surprise and delight she opened her eyes and became wide awake. My immediate assessment of the severity of her injury was wrong but my intuitive awareness that a problem existed and that my presence was needed proved to be correct. As a consequence I have learned to give greater credence to seemingly illogical impulses.

## Prayer and guidance

There is, as far as I know, no direct relationship between the Resurrection of Jesus and prayer, but it seems reasonable in a book dealing with the former to say something about the latter, and to mention the times when I found prayer to be a significant factor in crisis situations, particularly when individuals were close to death. I am not a man given to much prayer and my prayer life, such as it is, tends to be quiet and unspoken. The extempore spoken prayer of public worship is not my natural metier; I am more comfortable with the injunction given to the psalmist to 'Be still and know that I am God' and readily accept that it is in the prayer of contemplation that one comes closest to the Lord and is most strengthened by him. Having said that, it is the 'arrow prayers' that I have used in moments of crisis that have been answered most swiftly. Three incidents associated with such prayer come to mind. Each one took place when I was a General Practitioner working with three partners in Llanidloes, a small and ancient market town in the heart of Wales. Of central importance to the town was a cottage hospital which had been built as a memorial to the local men who had died in World War I. The hospital was staffed mainly by local people, and most pregnant women had their babies delivered there, often by people they had known from childhood. The chronically sick and the elderly had their own special unit, whilst consultants from the regional hospital at Aberystwyth visited on a regular basis to see people in the out-patient clinics. Graham Davies, my senior partner, made a point of being present when his patients were seeing a consultant, and the rest of us did so to a varying extent.

On one occasion, I was talking to Graham and the consultant surgeon Dick Isaac in the matron's office, when I had a strong feeling that I should not be there. Not knowing quite what to do, I sent up an arrow prayer seeking guidance and almost immediately afterwards regretted having done so, for I felt impelled to go to a house I had never previously visited where the residents were patients of another partner, Tom Britain. I felt foolish, but having sought guidance I realized that I must go to the house or not use that form of prayer again. It was a terrace house occupied by a 60-something-year-old lady and her 90-year-old aunty. On reaching the house, I was surprised to find the front door open but I walked in, as one could in those days, and finding no-one downstairs, went up the stairs which faced the front door. The top flight of the staircase gave access to two rooms and I looked first into the small room on the right. It was almost completely filled by a bed, in which lay an old woman *in extremis*. She died within a few moments of my entering the room and then, almost immediately afterwards, her niece returned from the shops and was very surprised to find me in the house. She said that 'Aunty', as she called her, seemed her usual self when she went to the shops just a few steps away, and there was nothing to indicate that she would take such a dramatic turn for the worse. She was very pleased that I had called in and was with the old lady when she died and that she had not been alone. I did nothing noteworthy but I was there at the moment of death. This may seem of no consequence but Dame Cicely Saunders, the charismatic founder of the Hospice movement, always emphasized the need for someone to be present at a deathbed because the terminally ill are frightened by the possibility of dying alone, and need to be assured that someone is with them. I cannot say why the impulse to visit the house came to me or why I followed it, but I am pleased I went and the niece was delighted that I was with her aunt at such a crucial moment. Later, when she decided to give me a memento of her aunt, she brought me the old lady's family Bible, which I still possess.

## Survival

This next incident involved an elderly lady who lived in Dol-llys, a residential home for old people run by the local authority in Powys, mid-Wales. It was past midnight and I was in bed when the matron of Dol-llys phoned and asked me to visit, so I crawled out of bed, donned the red track suit that I wore on such occasions and drove to Dol-llys where the matron was waiting in the entrance hall. She was a most pleasant and efficient lady and together we went up an old spiral staircase to the room that the sick woman occupied. As soon as I saw her it was obvious that she was desperately ill. She was cyanosed and breathless, and could not be roused. Immediate, life-saving treatment was necessary so I gave her what I had in the bag: an intravenous injection of aminophylline – an effective emergency treatment for heart failure, asthma and bronchospasm. Her condition did not improve; instead it deteriorated rapidly. She become deeply unconscious and vomited quantities of blackish fluid, which is a most undesirable complication when a person is unconscious. We dragged her onto her side – a standard procedure which meant that she could expel the vomit onto the floor instead of inhaling it into her lungs. Eventually the situation quietened; we cleaned her up and made her as comfortable as possible, then I sat on the bed and held her hand, knowing that she would die. In the quietness of my heart I prayed – not that she would recover, but that her soul would be acceptable to God. Then we left the room and I remember saying to the matron as I left the building: 'Phone me in the morning,' and thinking as I did so, that is when I will be giving you her death certificate. She telephoned during my morning surgery and as soon as I heard her voice I said, 'I'll bring the certificate along to you.'

'There's no need,' she replied, 'she's perfectly well now.'

The old lady had made a complete recovery and I remember seeing her just one more time before leaving the area. I happened to be in Dol-llys visiting another patient, and there she was standing at the top of the staircase smiling down at me. We did not speak and I left the area soon afterwards. It is possible that the aminophylline cured her, but I think not.

## Resuscitation of the dead

When I published an account of the next incident in the *British Medical Journal,* I was careful not to mention the significant role that prayer played as events progressed. In contrast to the two previous incidents, this was not a brief encounter but one that unfolded over a period of a week, and was almost melodramatic in its development. It took place in 1963, during the coldest winter of the 20th century in the UK, when the hills were covered with snow and many roads, including the one to Bronglais Hospital in Aberystwyth, were blocked and impassable. It began on a Saturday morning. This was the busiest day of the week for the Llanidloes doctors as it was market day, when the farmers brought their wives into town to shop and some used the opportunity to drop into the surgery to see the doctor and meet their friends. On this particular Saturday, I was scheduled to hold five surgeries and would also see patients in the cottage hospital and deal with any transient casualties.

I was about to start the first surgery when the receptionist told me that an urgent request had just arrived for me to visit an 80-year-old man who had severe chest pain. He lived some six miles away in the hills, at a farm called Hafodffraith. The waiting room was almost empty, so I decided to see the few patients seated there before visiting Mr Davies. But other people kept drifting in and by the time they were all seen, I was scheduled to hold a surgery in Caersws, some six miles in the opposite direction from the farm. I decided to go to Caersws first, and had just finished that surgery when a telephone message arrived to say the situation was desperate. I left immediately, travelling as fast as I could and as I did so I prayed, not aloud but with inward intensity, that he would be alive when I arrived. The urgency of the situation became more apparent when I drove off the paved road onto the farm track and found Mr Davies' neighbour, Mr Jones of Ystradolwen, holding a gate open to facilitate my passage.

This was my first visit to Hafodffraith, and as soon as I reached the farmhouse I knew the man was dead. It was apparent from the stance of the middle-aged man (his nephew) who stood outside the entrance door. I passed him without a word to find my suspicion confirmed by the body language of the old lady (his sister) who sat huddled by the kitchen fire. Again, no words were spoken and I went immediately upstairs and straight into Mr Davies' bedroom. He was not alone in the room; a middle-aged woman (his niece) stood by the door, gazing at the inert body lying on the bed. He was obviously dead, so I asked her for how long he had been like that and whether it been less than three minutes. She nodded her assent. I then went to the body, confirmed that he was dead and began external cardiac massage, intending to supplement this with mouth-to-mouth breathing. However, within a few moments he started to breathe spontaneously and his heart began to beat by itself! My sense of relief was enormous, even though he remained unconscious.

Now I had a new problem to resolve: how best to care for him. Normally I would have admitted him to the cottage hospital but all the beds were filled. The other alternative would have been to send him to Bronglais Hospital in Aberystwyth, but the road was blocked by snow. There was no choice but to keep him at home, so I placed him in the recovery position, raised the foot of the bed onto a chair, gave him an injection of chloramphenicol and told the family that I would send the district nurse as soon as possible. I then left to deal with my other surgeries and patients.

When I returned that evening, he was beginning to regain consciousness and by the next morning he was fully alert and smoking his pipe. We were all delighted at his recovery, though my own pleasure was tainted by less altruistic thoughts. Many people know that the Old Testament contains accounts of the dead being resuscitated by chest compression and mouth-to-mouth breathing, but this mode of resuscitation was not used by health workers in the first half of the twentieth century and some people actively opposed it. I remember being taught as a medical student not to use positive pressure techniques in the resuscitation of the newborn and was surprised when I saw Dr Tony Paddon resuscitate a new-born child in Labrador by blowing into her mouth. Moreover, he said that he had always used this technique and that it had always been successful. It was not until the 1960s that external cardiac massage and mouth-to-mouth respiration were shown to be an effective means of reviving the apparently dead and became generally accepted and widely practised. Workers in hospitals were beginning to report the successful revival of moribund patients using this method, but nothing similar had been demonstrated in a domiciliary situation nor in anyone as old as Mr Davies. I was sure he had had a coronary thrombosis and had sent blood to the laboratory to test this assumption. I was looking forward to receiving the report and then publishing an account of this unusual recovery in the medical press.

The week passed by uneventfully and we were all delighted with Mr Davies' progress. The family was happy and he seemed remarkably cheerful. The next Saturday was a sparkling day. The sun shone, everything glistened, and the postman brought the eagerly-awaited result of the blood test. It showed a high cardiac enzyme level, confirming the likelihood that his 'death' had been due to a coronary thrombosis. As on the previous Saturday, I completed my first surgery and went to Caersws where I saw the attending patients before driving to Hafodffraith. This time my mood was elated rather than anxious and prayerful, but it quickly changed when I entered the farmyard and saw the nephew standing in a forlorn manner outside the front door. I realized immediately that the old man was dead, and my suspicion was once again confirmed when I saw how miserable the sister looked as she sat on the settle by the fireside. I entered the bedroom and saw his lifeless body on the bed. On this occasion the woman standing in the room was not the niece but the district nurse, and again I enquired if he had been dead for more that three minutes. Even though the answer was no, I made no attempt to resuscitate him on this occasion. This was an instant decision that is difficult to rationalise over the years, but it was probably one I made because I felt that fate had intervened in a meaningful way. I felt that the man's death should now be accepted and I was glad that the family had at least been spared the trauma of an autopsy.

The need to make such a decision poses an ethical question that merits consideration. Would Jesus have restored Lazarus to life again if his friend had died once more before the Crucifixion?

CHAPTER 2

# Jesus Crucified

THE EVIDENCE SUPPORTING THE view that life persists
after death is cross-cultural and universal. It has been of
interest to psychiatrists and psychologists since the 1960s, most
notably among those concerned with deathbed and near-death
experiences, and with widowed peoples' continued perceptions
of their dead spouse. The death of Mr Davies of Hafodffraith (see
Chapter 1) left pertinent questions unanswered. For instance, we
do not know if he had a deathbed or a near-death experience in
which he saw Jesus or some other loved person. Nor do we know
if he had an out-of-body experience and was able to watch his
lifeless body being resuscitated. When he recovered consciousness,
he made no mention of any such happenings. However, he was
never questioned about the possibility and such events are rarely
reported unless the percipient is asked about them. Whatever
experiences Mr Davies may or may not have had during the
cardiac arrest, he was remarkably cheerful and at ease with himself
when he regained consciousness. He did not question what had
happened and accepted the situation as it was.

Mr Davies' resuscitation brings to mind the raising of Lazarus
by Jesus around 2000 years ago – an incident which raises further
questions. For instance, did Lazarus' restoration to life have a time
limit? We can give no clear answer to this question but one thing
is sure: his sisters, Martha and Mary, would have experienced an
enormous sense of relief at their brother's deliverance, though for
how long this uplift of mood continued cannot be ascertained.

Nor do we know the length of time that Lazarus survived.

There are other uncertainties. Was Lazarus among the holy people who Matthew says came out of their graves when Jesus died and entered Jerusalem after his Resurrection? What happened to them afterwards? These events are recorded in Matthew's Gospel (27: 51-53) but Church leaders offer no answers to the dilemmas they raise, so we are left to speculate. But if we do so, we need to examine as carefully as possible the realities upon which those reports, and Christian belief, are based.

The evidence that death is not the end of human life but rather a new birth is, according to Christian teaching, to be found in the life, death and Resurrection of Jesus of Nazareth – a Jew who lived in Palestine 2000 years ago and who was crucified when he was about thirty years old. Jesus was a peripatetic teacher who clashed with the Jewish leaders of his time and was arraigned before the courts on a charge of treason. He was found guilty under Roman law of claiming to be a king, and was publicly executed by crucifixion. His life and death might have been forgotten soon afterwards but for the remarkable occurrences that followed. People began to say that even though Jesus had been publicly slain and buried, he had survived death and had reappeared in bodily form. What is more, they said he appeared in this way on a number of occasions – sometimes to one or two individuals, at other times to many simultaneously. These events occurred over a relatively short period of time and were followed by the Ascension, his disappearance in the sight of his followers into heaven. These are not only Christian beliefs; some of these events are also found in the teachings of Islam, for Muslims hold Jesus in high esteem and believe that he was born miraculously, was a great prophet and worker of miracles, and probably entered heaven in bodily form. However, Muslims deny the Christian assertion that Jesus is the Son of God, regarding this belief as blasphemous. They also say that he did not die on the cross but survived the Crucifixion.

## Who was Jesus?

Remarkably little is known about the life of Jesus. Most of our knowledge is provided by accounts that were written at least thirty years after his death, probably between the years 65-95 CE. These accounts are recorded in the Gospels, the first four books of the New Testament. Further insights are provided by Jewish rabbinical teachings on the Messiah, prophetic passages in the Old Testament, and in the Epistles and the two other books that complete the New Testament. In the Gospels, we are told that Jesus was the son of a carpenter, that he was born miraculously, and that his parents fled with him to Egypt when he was a baby because the local ruler, King Herod, intended to kill him. We know that Jesus became a peripatetic teacher of great wisdom, that he was a healer and astounded people by his miraculous deeds. We also know that he was regarded by his followers as the eagerly awaited Messiah of Jewish expectations and this, together with the inference that he was the Son of God, so infuriated the religious leaders of his day that he was put to death.

Some people cast doubt on the historical reality of Jesus. For instance, they point out that none of the reports we possess about Jesus are likely to have been written by an eyewitness. That is fair comment and Christian theologians would probably not dispute it, but the Gospel writers would certainly have been in contact with people who had known Jesus and been present at important stages of his life. There is also non-biblical evidence to substantiate the reports given in the New Testament about the life of Jesus. For instance, Christianity's growth in adversity and its existence as a worldwide Church provides supportive evidence for the claim that Jesus was a real person who lived in Palestine 2000 years ago. Documentary evidence is provided by the Jewish historian Flavius Josephus (37 CE – c.100 CE), who refers to Jesus in his book *Antiquities of the Jews* as follows:

Now there was about this time Jesus, a wise man, if it be

lawful to call him a man, for he was a doer of wonderful works, a teacher of such men as receive the truth with pleasure. He drew over to him both many of the Jews and many of the Gentiles. He was [the] Christ. And when Pilate, at the suggestion of the principal men amongst us, had condemned him to the cross, those that loved him at the first did not forsake him, for he appeared to them alive again the third day; as the divine prophets had foretold these and ten thousand other wonderful things concerning him. And the tribe of Christians, so named from him, are not extinct at this day. [1]

Flavius' account, known as the *Testimonium Flavium*, has the added relevance of being written by a Jew who lived in Palestine soon after the death of Jesus. Josephus accepted Roman citizenship but retained his Jewish identity and did not convert to the Christian faith.

The Roman historian Tacitus also referred briefly to Jesus. [2] However, outside the Christian tradition, the most important indication of the historical reality of Jesus is the significance given to him by Muslims. This is most clearly shown in the *Holy Qur'an* which, in my copy, contains twenty references to Jesus in the index. Only two other individuals, Moses and Muhammad, are listed more often.

Jesus was a man of his time. His clothes, habitation, food, coinage and means of transport would have been very different from the social conditions in present-day Israel and Palestine. His education would have been radically different from that of today and his understanding of the physical nature of the universe, of human physiology, of the underlying causes of disease and the best methods to cultivate the land would bear little resemblance to present beliefs and practices. But that does not mean that we can dismiss the most important claim for him, that he is the Son of God and the Saviour of mankind. Whether this is true or not is a matter of conjecture and belief, and largely dependent on the

28

reality of the Resurrection – his reappearance in physical form and ability to communicate with his followers shortly after being publicly executed. His Resurrection was essential to confirm not just the prophetic expectations of the Jewish people for the coming of the Messiah, but also his own claim that he must experience great sufferings and be rejected by the elders, chief priests and doctors of the law, and that he would be killed and rise again three days later. (Mark 8: 31-32.)

## The Crucifixion

An important difference between Christianity and Islam is that Muslims believe that Jesus did not die on the cross – an assertion that is specifically stated in the *Qur'an* in *Surah 4*. It is imperative, therefore, that we look closely at what happened when Jesus was crucified and consider the medical evidence that would help us to reach a conclusion.

It was customary in Jesus' day for all condemned criminals to be flogged before execution. The whip used consisted of four or five leather thongs braided with lead balls and pieces of sheep bones which would have caused deep lacerations penetrating through the full thickness of the skin. The number of strokes given is not known but one third had to be given on the chest and the remainder on the back with the victim bending forward. [3] After being flogged, Jesus was taken to the soldiers' headquarters to act as a plaything for the troops – a custom that was granted to them only once a year. There he became the centre of jocular ribaldry, was garlanded with a crown of thorns and beaten over the head with a stick. In some translations of the original Greek text this stick is called a reed, but the rod used was probably much more heavy than just a single reed. The Greek word for a reed was *kulamos*, but this included anything made from reeds and could mean a rod, arrow or writing material. Consequently, the blows

Jesus received on his head were more substantial than is generally realized, and would have driven the thorns that covered his head deeply into his scalp and forehead.

Like all condemned men, Jesus was required to carry the cross-piece of the cross to the place of execution. The distance covered is not known, but we do know that he was too weak to do this unaided. Condemned men were usually able to perform this task on their own, but it is possible the extra abuse he received from the soldiers prevented him from carrying it out alone. At the place of execution, he was stripped and placed on the ground with the cross-piece beneath him so that the nails could be hammered into his forearms above the wrists. The cross-piece, with Jesus attached, was then raised on to the vertical section of the cross and attached to a tenon. Jesus' knees were then twisted sideways and his legs nailed – probably between the tibia and Achilles tendon or through the heel bones – into the wood. Suspended in this way, his buttocks would have rested on a *sedile*, a supporting projection from the upright piece, and this would have raised his head about 18 inches above those of the bystanders. [4]

## Why did Jesus die so quickly?

Jesus died within nine hours of being attached to the cross. This was uncommon. Crucified men usually took three or four days to die, and we know that the two men crucified alongside Jesus had their legs broken by the soldiers to ensure they died before the Sabbath began. The soldiers standing nearby were certain that he had died, but Pontius Pilate was surprised to learn of his death and questioned the officer of the guard before allowing the body to be removed (Mark 15: 44). John's Gospel says that a spear was thrust into Jesus' side after he had died and that this produced an emission of blood and water, but some commentators doubt the veracity of this report because corpses do not bleed. It is possible, however, that fluid (hydrothorax) and/or blood (haemothorax) may have collected within the chest cavity whilst Jesus was alive and was released by the spear. This would have eased any breathing problems he may have had if, as Muslims believe, he was alive when removed from the cross.

The question of why Jesus died so quickly remains unanswered. Various explanations have been advanced but they all remain a matter of conjecture and no-one can be certain of the precise cause of death. Professor Benjamin Brenner, an Israeli academic, suggests that he died from pulmonary embolism. This is a common cause of sudden death especially when, as in Jesus' case, there has been preceding dehydration, immobilization and trauma. Brenner goes even further and says that pulmonary embolism was probably the most frequent cause of death by crucifixion. He says that Jesus' genetic inheritance may have given him a hyper-coagulable condition that would increase the likelihood of his developing a deep vein thrombosis and pulmonary emboli. This genetic mutation is common in Israel today, especially in people who live in the Galilee area. [5] A simpler explanation is suggested by Professor Murphy-O'Connor, who says that Jesus died so quickly because he had lost so much blood. [6] Both these suggestions are helpful but neither explains why other crucified victims from the area survived longer than Jesus did.

Whatever the immediate cause of death, we know that Jesus suffered more physical abuse from the soldiers than the two men who were crucified with him. He was already exhausted by his vigil in the Garden of Gethsemane, and this would have weakened him physically before he was imprisoned, ill-treated and crucified. Eventually he would reach a state of clinical shock with a low blood pressure, and this would have been exacerbated by the continual blood loss caused by the scourging and bleeding from the scalp. Whilst suspended on the cross, the oxygen supply to his brain would have become minimal. There is no doubt that when he died, or appeared to have died, the guards believed he was dead. Having said that, instances do occur of medically competent people declaring a person dead who subsequently proves to be alive.

Even more remarkable are the recorded cases of crucifixions where people were taken down from the cross whilst still alive and surviving the ordeal. Flavius Josephus recorded such a case following the Jewish revolt against Rome (66-73 C.E.):

> When I was sent by Titus to a village called Thecoa I saw many captives crucified, and remembered three of them as my former acquaintances. I was very sorry for them, and went with tears in my eyes to Titus and told him of them, so he immediately commanded them to be taken down, and to have the greatest care taken of them, in order to aid their recovery: yet two of them died under the physician's hands, while the third recovered. [7]

## Did Jesus die on the cross?

The two criminals who were crucified alongside Jesus had their legs broken to ensure their rapid death from asphyxia, and there can be no doubt that they died on the cross. However, Jesus did not have his legs broken, so this absolute certainty does not apply to him. Consequently, it must be said that the historical records provide no conclusive proof that Jesus died on the cross. It is likely that he did, but from a modern perspective it is a matter of faith rather than proven fact. It is a belief that millions of people, including Muslims and sceptics, reject. Islam's 1.4 billion adherents believe that whilst Jesus may appear to have been dead when he was removed from the cross, he was actually alive and was resuscitated by his followers. Any possibility that Jesus died on the cross is denied explicitly in the *Holy Qur'an*, where verse 157 of *Surah* 4 states:

That they said (in boast)
'We killed Christ Jesus
The son of Mary,
The messenger of Allah,'
But they killed him not,
Nor crucified him,
But so it was made to appear to them,
And those who differ therein are full of doubts,
With no certain knowledge,
With only conjectures to follow,
For of a surety they killed him not. [8]

Some early Christian gnostic sects, including the Basilidians and Docetae, also thought that Jesus did not die at Calvary. The Basilidians said that another person had been substituted for Jesus, while the Docetae believed that Jesus was fully divine and in no sense human. Because of his divinity, the Docetae said that Jesus could not be sullied with human flesh and never had a physical body, only a spiritual body; consequently his Crucifixion was not real, only apparent. There were other controversies within the early Christian communities which the Church leaders had to resolve, but eventually a measure of agreement was reached, in 325 C.E. at an Ecumenical Council summoned to Nicaea by the Emperor Constantine. There an agreed statement of faith, the Nicene Creed, was produced and Arianism, then a prominent Christian sect which denied the divinity of Christ, was condemned as heretical.

Theological disputes have been a constant factor within the Christian Church since its early days. The nature of Christ's resurrected body is uncertain, with current leading clergy expressing differing views. Some hold to the doctrine that Christ appeared in his human physical form, others that it was probably a spiritual body, whilst others express uncertainty or even more radical ideas. These conflicting opinions are discussed *inter alia* in the section dealing with the beliefs and experiences of Anglican bishops. Before that, we shall consider the historical evidence for the reality of Christ's Resurrection.

# CHAPTER 3

# Resurrection

JESUS' RESURRECTION FROM THE dead is central to the Christian belief that there is life after death. This belief will be considered from two aspects: Jesus' post-Resurrection appearances to the people who knew him well; and the post-Ascension appearances – the encounters that followed his ascent into heaven. Of the latter, the best known example is his meeting with Saul on the road to Damascus, but similar encounters have been reported by people up to the present day.

The first recorded account of the Resurrection is provided by St Paul in a letter he wrote about 20 years after the death of Jesus to his friends in Corinth. Paul's comments were brief but are considered of the utmost importance to Christians. In the letter, he named three groups of people and three individuals who had met the resurrected Jesus:

> I handed on to you the facts which had been imparted to me: that Christ had died for our sins, in accordance with the scriptures; that he was buried; that he was raised to life on the third day, according to the scriptures; and that he appeared to Cephas, and afterwards to the Twelve. Then he appeared to over five hundred of our brothers at once, most of whom are still alive, although some have died. Then he appeared to James, and afterwards to all the apostles. In the end he appeared even to me. It was like an abnormal birth.' ( 1 Corinthians 15: 5-8. *The New English Bible.*)

In this brief paragraph, Paul asserted that Christ's death and Resurrection were not chance happenings but events that had been foretold hundreds of years earlier in the Jewish scriptures.

Moreover, it was Paul's firm belief that those prophecies had been fulfilled by the death and Resurrection of Jesus.

In depicting the life of Jesus, the Gospels provide eleven instances of his Resurrection appearances. These show how the crucified Jesus appeared to his followers not as a ghost, a majestic figure or a dazzling light, but as an ordinary person who at first glance could be mistaken for someone else. His appearing to the disciples in a recognizable human form is the most striking aspect of the Resurrection and differs markedly from the post-Ascension encounters recorded by Luke in the Acts of the Apostles. But similar appearances have been recorded subsequently and are reported in Chapters 6 to 9, where we consider the claims made by people who believe they have met the risen Jesus in recent years.

Women were the first witnesses of the Resurrection. The Gospels name them as Mary Magdalene, Mary mother of James, Joanna, Salome, and the mother of Zebedee's sons. The very first person to see the risen Jesus was probably Mary Magdalene (Mark 16: 9). Her immediate reaction, and those of the women with her, was to hurry to the disciples and tell them the good news, but the men did not believe them. Such initial scepticism is understandable because the news the women brought was so unbelievable. Other factors might have affected the men's response. They were 'sick' with grief and fearful for their own safety (John 20: 19), and the social distinctions that existed between men and women at that time may have made the women's report seem even less credible.

## The narratives

Jesus was first seen by the women who were closest to him. In Matthew's account, Mary Magdalene and the other Mary were walking to the tomb when they felt a violent earthquake and saw an angel who told them to go to the disciples and tell them that Jesus had risen from the dead. This they did, meeting Jesus on the way and prostrating themselves at his feet (Matthew 28: 1-9). Mark gives a similar account of a meeting by the tomb, this time involving three women (Mark 16: 1-8). He also mentions other instances: Jesus walking in the countryside with two men and his sudden appearance to the Eleven when they were eating, and how he had reproached them for not believing the reports that he had risen from the dead.

John's Gospel says that Jesus appeared to Mary Magdalene when she was weeping outside the tomb. She did not recognize him at first, not even after he spoke to her, but when she realized that it was Jesus, he told her not to hold on to him but to go to his brothers with her news. This Gospel also contains an account of Jesus appearing to the disciples when they were in a locked room and how he admonished Thomas because he required physical proof that Jesus was alive (John 20: 10-29).

Luke's account of the women's visit to the tomb is brief. In it they are not said to have met Jesus but two men (angels) who terrified them. Despite their fear, the women listened to the angels' account of Jesus' Resurrection and took the news to the disciples, who did not believe them (Luke 24: 1-12). Luke's Gospel also provides the most detailed report of any meeting with the risen Jesus. This was the encounter on the road to Emmaus, when Jesus came alongside two men who were walking to the village. He spoke to them and they invited him to spend the night with them, but it was only when he broke bread at their evening meal that they recognized him (Luke 24: 13-34). This meeting has features reminiscent of Dr McAll's encounter with Jesus in Northern China during the 1930s (discussed in Chapter 8).

The four Gospels contain other accounts of Jesus' Resurrection appearances. Among them is the occasion when he appeared suddenly to the Eleven disciples and terrified them because they thought he was a ghost. To calm their fears, he asked for something to eat, and they gave him a piece of fish which he ate in front of them (Luke 24: 36-43). The fear and disbelief shown by the disciples on this and other occasions is an important reminder that belief in the Resurrection stories does not always come easily, and that Jesus' disciples have provided modern sceptics with important role models for their uncertainty.

## The disciples' grief

The death of Jesus was an enormous blow to his followers. Their guiding light and hope for the future had been killed in a most distressing and public manner. Two thousand years later, it is difficult to fully appreciate the disciples' mood and state of mind following this loss, but the fact that we now have a better understanding of the psychology and the processes associated with bereavement is helpful. We know from the many studies on bereavement undertaken since World War II that the disciples' immediate reaction to the death of Jesus would probably have been a sense of numbness, disbelief and inner emptiness. They would probably have been confused, tearful and restless – unable to accept the reality of what had happened. This disbelief is likely to have been associated with an overpowering sense of anger. We also know that they were afraid (John 20: 19).

Fear for their own safety is one reason the men stayed indoors. This would explain the women being the first to visit the tomb and meet Jesus. They may have felt at less risk out of doors than the men, being perhaps less easily recognized as a member of Jesus' group. Another possible explanation for the men's seclusion is that they were observing the Jewish mourning customs of that time, which are likely to have resembled those kept by Jews today. If this is so, the disciples would have begun their grief work with *Shiva,* a seven-day period of family reunion in which no tasks are undertaken and only certain parts of the scriptures read. The house would have been lit continuously by candles, mirrors would have been covered and the mourners would have been seated on low stools. For the first three days, the grief-stricken disciples would not have greeted people nor replied to them, and the daily prayers would not have been said. This would have been the beginning of a thirty-day mourning period during which the gradual change from the sadness of bereavement to the resumption of a more normal life would have taken place.

## The disciples' reaction to Jesus' appearance

Once the disciples had accepted the reality of Jesus' Resurrection, the normal grieving process would have ceased and an entirely new situation needed to be dealt with. One imagines that relief and happiness would have been the disciples' immediate response, but this is not the reaction recorded in the Gospels. They remained withdrawn and uncertain until Pentecost, when their attitude changed remarkably. Their lacklustre response to wonderful news reminds me of a widow who was referred for hospice care with terminal cancer of the stomach. After a few weeks of hospice care, her condition improved so remarkably that the diagnosis was reviewed and proved to be erroneous. A large benign ulcer of the stomach had been wrongly diagnosed as cancerous, and the widow and her bachelor son were confronted with new problems. They had accepted and prepared themselves for her imminent death and suddenly had to adjust to the realization that her life expectation would be much longer. When they learnt of the changed prognosis, the expected mood of euphoria did not manifest itself. They were quietly pleased but had new uncertainties to confront. It is possible that the disciples would have reacted in a similar way when they accepted the reality of Jesus' Resurrection. The Gospel accounts of their responses to the Resurrection differ in detail but their main reactions can be listed as follows:

| Clasped his feet | Matthew 28: 9 |
| Did not recognize him | Luke 24: 13-29; John 20: 14-16 |
| Disbelief | Mark 16: 9-15; Luke 24: 11; John 20: 25 |
| Fear | Mark 16: 8; Luke 24: 37; John 20: 19 |
| Hearts on fire | Luke 24: 32 |
| Joy | John 20: 20 |
| Not convinced | Luke 24: 41 |
| Recognized him | John 21: 7 |
| Thought he was a ghost | Luke 24: 37 |
| Told others | Luke 24: 35; John 20: 10-18 |

The most frequently reported reactions were disbelief, fear and a failure to recognize him.

## Importance of the Resurrection

The importance of the Resurrection for Christians cannot be overstated. A bishop stated this clearly in a letter to me when he wrote: 'To me, belief in the Resurrection of Our Lord Jesus Christ is central to Christian belief. 'If Christ is not risen our Faith is in vain'.'

The time span of Jesus' Resurrection appearances is not known, but they probably occurred over a relatively short period – perhaps a few days or weeks. During this time he appeared in human form to his friends and was able to share in their everyday activities; talking with them, walking, eating with them and lighting a fire for them. He appeared on at least eleven occasions to individuals, small groups of people and once to a crowd of about 500 people. Most surprisingly, those who knew him well were often slow to recognize him, and he also had a disconcerting way of appearing and disappearing unexpectedly. After the Ascension, Jesus appeared to Stephen and Paul in three other ways which are recorded in the Acts of the Apostles:

1   In a vision to Stephen, shortly before his death(Acts 7: 55-57).

2   To Saul on the road to Damascus (Acts 9: 3-6; 22: 6-9; 26: 12-16).

3   In a vision to Paul when he was in a trance (Acts 22: 17-21).

Jesus' ability to appear in different locations and at various times, seems not to have been restricted by time or space. This has been made clear by the reports given in the New Testament. We are also told, by those who have had such experiences, that Jesus continues to appear to people today – sometimes as a vision, occasionally in a more discernible human form. This phenonenom will be explored in Sections 2 and 3.

## Post-Ascension appearances

Jesus' meeting with Saul on the road to Damascus is the best known of the post-Ascension encounters. It is a meeting that differs from the Gospel stories in a number of key points: Saul's experience was visionary; he did not see a human figure; he did not walk alongside Jesus or share food with him; and there was no physical presence that he could touch. Instead, he saw a light from the sky that was 'more brilliant than the sun', shining around him and his companions as they travelled towards Damascus (Acts 26: 13-14). They all fell to the ground and Saul heard a voice speaking in the Jewish language which asked, 'Why do you persecute me, Saul?' Saul replied, 'Who are you, Lord?' and received the reply: 'I am Jesus, whom you are persecuting. Get up and go into the city, and you will be told what you must do.' (Acts 9: 4-6.)

We do not know if Saul's companions heard the voice or whether the words meant anything to them, but we do know that Saul was blinded by the light. This is significant for being the only recorded instance in which a person was injured by Jesus. Being blind, Saul could not walk unaided and had to be led into Damascus, where he refused to eat or drink for three days. After this time, Ananias came to heal and comfort him, and Saul was baptised and changed his name to Paul. These events were recorded by Luke in three separate passages in the book of Acts, and we are fortunate to have his reports as Paul's own accounts are almost totally lacking in detail. His letter to the Corinthians contains a remarkably brief account of Jesus' appearances, ending with the comment: 'and last of all he appeared to me also. It was like an abnormal birth.' (1 Corinthians 15: 3-8.) Paul was equally reticent in his letter to the Galatians, saying only that 'God, who had set me apart from birth and called me by his grace, chose to reveal his Son to me' (Galatians 1: 15-16).

## Other visions

Both the Old and New Testaments speak of visions. Some involve angelic beings, others tell of dazzling lights and commanding voices. The Old Testament tells us that God spoke to Moses from a burning bush (Exodus 3: 2-5) and that the Glory of God covered and filled the Tabernacle and guided the people of Israel on their journeys (Exodus 40: 34-36). In the New Testament, the women who went to anoint Jesus at the tomb were confronted by an earthquake and by men whose appearance and clothes were like lightning (Matthew 28: 2-3; Luke 24: 4). At the Transfiguration, Peter, James and John saw Elijah and Moses talking with Jesus, whose clothes had become dazzling white; and they heard a voice speaking from a cloud that said, 'This is my Son, whom I love. Listen to him.' (Mark 9: 2-7.)

Paul's encounter with Jesus outside Damascus was the first to be recorded between them, but others took place with important consequences. These include the occasion when Paul went to the Temple to pray, fell into a trance and had a vision of Jesus, who told him to leave Jerusalem and go and preach to the Gentiles. At first Paul demurred, claiming that people would recognize him as the man who had persecuted Christians and had been present at Stephen's death, but in the end he did what he was told.

## Life after death

The message Paul preached to the Gentiles was that Jesus of Nazareth had been crucified outside Jerusalem, that he had risen from the dead and was the 'first fruits of the harvest of the dead'. This teaching was in line with the belief held by many Jews at that time, especially by the Pharisees (of whom Paul had been one), that when the long-awaited Messiah appeared on earth, the Jewish dead would arise out of their graves and their role as God's chosen people would be vindicated. Paul believed that this expectation had been inaugurated and fulfilled by Jesus – a belief that was later supported by Matthew's report that when Jesus died, 'the bodies of many holy people who had died, came out of their tombs and were raised to life.' (Matthew 27: 50-53.)

Paul's thinking on the Resurrection of the dead was probably based on more than traditional Jewish teachings. He was an educated man who had been raised in the Greek city of Tarsus and would have been familiar with the varied philosophies and religious beliefs of that time. He would have heard people talk about the nature of the soul and the afterlife, and on the existence of a spiritual body that some people equated with the soul but which others regarded as a separate entity that provided a body for the soul in the afterlife. In his letters, Paul wrote often of the Resurrection but said little about the physical Resurrection of the dead. This is a surprising omission for a Pharisee. Instead, he wrote eloquently about the mystery of death and of the afterlife, stating quite clearly that 'flesh and blood cannot inherit the kingdom of God' (1 Corinthians 16: 50) and emphasising that victory over death has been gained 'through our Lord Jesus Christ'.

The nature of the afterlife, whether it is physical or spiritual, seems not to have concerned Paul very much. In that sense his position was typically Jewish, an attitude which Professor Louis Ginsberg explained in this way:

> The Rabbis often speak of the reward awaiting the righteous after their death as consisting not in material pleasure but in enjoying divine glory. Nevertheless, the development of the religious thought of the Jew shows a marked tendency to fix the centre of gravity of religion not in a thought of the world beyond but rather to fasten and establish it in the actual life of man on earth. [1]

That seems to have been Paul's position. He was less interested in discussing the nature of the afterlife than in establishing a relationship with Christ in the present moment, and in teaching the Gospel message of forgiveness, Resurrection and of a new life available to everyone in Christ, now and for eternity.

## Comment/Summary

This chapter has provided a brief review of Jesus' Resurrection and of its immediate affect on his close followers. The disciples were devastated by Jesus' public Crucifixion, and their immediate reactions were grief and fear. They remained indoors, secluded from other people, maybe because they were observing Jewish mourning customs or perhaps because they were too frightened to venture outside. Only Jesus' female followers seemed to have the courage and determination to visit his tomb to anoint his body, and it was they who had the first meetings with him. Yet their encounters with Jesus were not mentioned by Paul in his account of those first meetings with the risen Jesus. He mentioned men by name and included his own post-Ascension encounter, but said nothing of the women's involvement.

Spontaneous joy was not the disciples' immediate response when they learned of Jesus' Resurrection or when they saw him for the first time since his death. Instead, disbelief, fear and a failure to recognize him were more usual reactions. Some even thought he was a ghost and Thomas demanded the most objective of proofs before he would relinquish his doubts. Similar attitudes persist today and people are rightly wary of being duped. So should we accept or reject the claims made by our contemporaries when they say they have met the risen Jesus in spirit and in flesh today? The next two sections will examine this question more closely.

# Section 2

# Bishops

CHAPTER 4

# Contacting the Bishops

THE ORIGINS OF THIS book can be traced back to the late
1960s when I undertook a study on the post-bereavement
experiences of widowed people and discovered that many
continued to enjoy a close relationship with their dead spouse,
sometimes for years. A brief account of this study was published
in the *British Medical Journal* [1] in 1971 and the full report was
presented to the University of London in 1971 as an MD thesis
which remains available to readers in the University's library.
Since then, the results have been replicated in other centres and
have entered the mainstream of psychiatric thinking and teaching.
More precisely, psychiatrists now accept the main findings that
almost 50 per cent of widowed people are aware, at times, of the
presence of their deceased spouse – some even seeing them – and
that this is a normal and helpful consequence of bereavement.

Although the study was widely reported in the medical
and secular press, over 30 years elapsed before theologians first
referred to the findings. Gerald O'Collins, Professor of Theology
at the Gregorian University in Rome, quoted from it in his book
*Easter Faith: Believing in the Risen Jesus*. This was pleasing because
it always seemed to me that the insights the study provided are
relevant to our understanding of the Resurrection and all that
followed. I came across Professor O'Collins' book in the review
section of *The Tablet* and, finding the article interesting, ordered
a copy by 'phone. When the book arrived I was surprised to find
the 1971 paper quoted quite extensively and, although pleased

that O'Collins wrote kindly of it, was interested in his concluding remark that 'we misrepresent matters if we allege a close and illuminating analogy' between the experiences of the disciples at the Resurrection and those of the bereaved today [2]. This analogy was not advanced in the original paper, which provided purely factual data about the experiences of the bereaved, but I do not discount its possibility and think that the idea is worth exploring and the implications discussed.

O'Collins offered two main reasons for discounting a possible relationship between the experiences of widowed people and those of the early disciples. His reasons and the issues they raise will be discussed in Chapter 11, but essentially they are:

1   The extraordinary public claims that Jesus made about his identity and mission.
2   No widowed person's life was changed so dramatically that they became missionaries, proclaiming to the world their experiences and what they implied.

There is, of course, a great difference in the significance of the post-Resurrection appearances and the experiences reported by widowed people, but a more realistic assessment of their perceptions would be helpful to the individuals concerned and to the Church Temporal, instead of simply dismissing them as of no theological significance. Reading *Easter Faith* was, therefore, an important catalyst in the writing of this book.

Another factor was relevant: I had become increasingly interested in the Resurrection (what elderly Christian could not be?) and had collected a small number of instances in which people claimed to have met the risen Jesus in ways similar to those reported in the New Testament. These accounts differed from the biblical ones in being contemporary and, in some instances, involved people I knew. It seemed reasonable to consider these alongside the biblical accounts and to reassess the latter from this enhanced perspective whilst still respecting the judgements reached by men in the past.

Placing current experiences of the risen Jesus alongside those recorded in a biblical setting is a relatively recent development among academics. Professor Phillip Wiebe did so in his book *Visions of Jesus* [3] in which he provides a critical assessment of the claims made by 28 contempories to have seen, met or spoken to the risen Jesus. A total of 36 meetings are reported by these 28 individuals; some occurring in complete consciousness, others in a trance or in a dream. In his analysis of these cases, Professor Wiebe categorised the people he interviewed into four distinct groups:

1 Trance and Dreamlike Experiences (4 cases)
This group consisted of people who had fallen into a trance or had dreamlike experiences, or whose experience seemed to start in the normal world but did not continue there.

2 Altered Environment Cases (5 cases)
These people experienced a significant change in the physical environment they knew themselves to be in.

3 Private Experiences (15 cases)
In this group the physical environment remained normal apart from the visionary figures that appeared in it.

4 Cases with Observable Effects (4 cases)
In this group several people were simultaneously affected, and it included instances in which two or more people apparently saw the same thing.

Weibe also listed a group of four cases which included people with whom he could conduct only brief and incomplete interviews; and two he could not contact directly but were well known to acquaintances of his. He also mentioned a sixth kind of vision;

one which was not described in detail by the percipient but was essentially a re-enactment of some event in the life of Christ, such as the Crucifixion or the flight to Egypt.

Professor Wiebe said that few studies had been undertaken into this important topic. As it was a field that warranted further study and was of interest to me, I decided to undertake my own investigations. I chose a three-track approach, seeking information from three separate sources. The first approach was to members of the Coventry Diocese – more specifically to about 1,500 people who attended an ordination service held in Coventry Cathedral on Sunday, 4 July 2004. Each person received a copy of the Cathedral newsletter with the order of service, and this contained a brief request asking them to contact me if they had had an experience of the risen Jesus comparable to those reported in the Gospels (see Appendix one). Not many people replied. A few friends sent messages of goodwill and one lady telephoned offering to send a written account of her experiences. This was the sort of response I was looking for, as it is more meaningful for people to write their own accounts than to be paraphrased during an interview.

The second approach was to members of the Coventry Diocesan Cursillo (see Appendix two for a copy of the letter). Started in Spain during the 1940s as a means of renewing the life of the Catholic Church, Cursillo is an international organisation with branches in the Catholic, Anglican and Free Churches which aims to strengthen the life of established Christians by means of residential weekends, house groups and regular meetings. There are about 300 Cursillistas in the Coventry diocese, out of which two replied. This was a good response and, although the sample size was small, suggests that about one in 150 Cursillistas believe that they have had a significant meeting with the risen Jesus and are willing to allow their encounters to be made known to the wider public. The letters they wrote are fascinating and these, together with the lady's account mentioned above, are discussed in Chapter 6.

The third approach was to retired bishops. While the response from lay people in the Coventry Diocese was illuminating and helpful, the bishops' replies were the most significant. Using *Crockfords Directory of Anglican Clergy* [4], I identified the 102 Honorary Assistant (retired) Bishops of the Church of England who were listed for the year 2003 and wrote to them with two requests: first, that they complete a short questionnaire and second, to give their views about the Resurrection and include any personal experience of Jesus – subjective or otherwise – that they might be willing to share with me and a wider audience if this book reached publication. In the event that their letters would be open to public scrutiny, the bishops were assured that their answers to the questionnaire would be regarded as confidential and used only for statistical purposes. As an additional safeguard, the identity of responders could not be established unless they themselves provided their names and addresses. (A copy of the letter and the questionnaire sent to the bishops is provided in appendices three and four.)

## Who to include?

Having chosen the assistant bishops as a target group, it soon became apparent that not all those listed in Crockford's could be included in the study. A relatively high proportion were too old and infirm to collaborate. Consequently, only those bishops under the age of 85 who lived in England were contacted. Letters were sent to 82 bishops and replies received from 67 – a response rate of 81.7%. This was a remarkably high return rate for a postal questionnaire. Some merely returned the questionnaire, others included relevant comments and some wrote quite long letters. The warmth of the letters was most encouraging and, in addition to good wishes, often included remarks such as:

A difficult but important area.

I hope your research uncovers something of real interest.

I was fascinated by your letter because, of course, I think you are onto something important.

I wish you well in your research and will be interested in the outcome.

Thank you for the work you are doing on this important, nay vital, subject.

The interest, warmth and kindness shown by the bishops was outstanding. Some replied despite having to cope with personal problems and tragedies. One bishop, who decided not to reply, sent a brief note to say that he had made a firm decision never to answer questionnaires. I felt a bond of sympathy with him, because immediately before opening his letter I had torn up a questionnaire with 140 questions plus biro, sent by a professional marketing firm. The thought *touché* came immediately.

## Why contact retired bishops?

This is a question that was sometimes raised. One bishop wrote: 'I am glad to answer your questions though I am baffled to understand why assistant bishops should be singled out. Surely Diocesans, Deans, Archdeacons and College Principals could be just as relevant.' The decision on who to contact within the Anglican hierarchy had, in fact, been considered very carefully. Assistant bishops, being mainly older men who had retired from more active roles, seemed the most likely to respond and able to provide the most interesting replies. They had a mass of experience to draw upon, would have thought deeply about the subject and would probably have had more time to consider the implications of the study and complete the questionnaire. The high response rate and the warmth of their replies gives some justification to that assessment. So, too, does the content of the letters, as the following indicate.

**Bishop 1.**

Thank you for your letter and its enclosed brief questionnaire. The completed questionnaire is enclosed. Please forgive me for not writing more fully about the Resurrection. Actually, the subject is very much in my mind at the moment – my wife died ten weeks ago after a prolonged period of suffering from cancer – but at the moment, I am rather preoccupied 'picking up the pieces' and supporting the family. However, the two sources of my reading in recent days have been Bishop Tom Wright's *Resurrection of the Son of God* and the writings of James Alison. They are both superb but I find Alison's perception of the Resurrection and its consequences not just for the individual but for the Church and the world very stimulating indeed.

I wish you well in your endeavour.

**Bishop 2.**

You must forgive me for not writing as to your second query. I am very old now and looking forward to myself being caught up in the Spirit – Spirit of God, Spirit of Christ. I can get as excited as Paul about all this, because without wishing to set out definitions, I believe strongly in the Resurrection to eternal life.

Yours sincerely,

This bishop made other comments which will be discussed in Chapter 5. The tone of his letter reinforced my impression that the Resurrection might be of more immediate concern to older clergy than perhaps it is to younger ones. Naturally, this possibility has not been tested properly as young clergy were not contacted, but it remains a strong impression. Whether it is true or false, an approach to retired bishops seemed more appropriate than an approach to clergy who are still fully engaged in the problems of overseeing the care of the church and its people.

## Even bishops have problems

It will be apparent from the extracts given above that the bishops have been remarkably open and generous in their responses. They have written most kindly and encouragingly despite personal problems and heartaches. Among the other letters received were the following comments:

**Bishop 3.**

I have read your letter with interest but I am afraid I may not be of much help to you. I enclose your questionnaire. Failing health makes it difficult to concentrate on the issues you are raising. In my ministry I have been much aware of the Holy Spirit, however described, rather than Jesus the man.

Sorry not to be of more help.

Best wishes with your project.

**Bishop 4.**

I hope you will forgive my responding very briefly to your kind letter but my wife has just suffered a major stroke and is in hospital. As a result I am rather preoccupied.

A very late reply carried the following note:

**Bishop 5.**

I am very sorry I have not returned this before. I had to undergo seven weeks of radiotherapy in the late spring and early summer. More recently I have been busy with schools. I am afraid it is a rather inadequate reply and now I am sure I am too late to enlarge a little upon it.

A bishop's son wrote:

I write on behalf of my father and thank you for your recent letter on his behalf. My father is currently completely physically debilitated and mentally impaired following a devastating stroke in July 2002. In consequence I am unable to communicate any of his views in response to your letter. I am however sure, that under normal circumstances, my father would wish you well in your research and every success for the publication of your book.

## Cultural diversity

A number of bishops suggested that the study should be extended to examine the way in which people's experience of the risen Christ is a product of their cultural background. The following letter makes this point and it is one that should be taken seriously, ideally by researchers with good access to people of diverse traditions and lifestyles. The letter also reveals most poignantly the vulnerability of bishops and members of their families to personal tragedies.

**Bishop 6.**

Thank you for your letter and details of the interesting research in which you are engaged. I return your questionnaire – hardly a big chore! I wonder about the wisdom of circulating it to retired bishops, who are an identifiable group, of course, but a bit monochrome – products of our further education system, articulate, white (apart from my former colleague W who has retired to Barbados).

In my experience as a priest in urban industrial areas here, and ten years in SE Africa, visionary experiences of Christ are much more frequent amongst people who either cannot read, or are not used to receiving necessary awareness/knowledge experience via the written word. The latter category includes most people in our big council estates or inner city areas. I have been told many such experiences which have been helpful, sometimes critical, in people's lives, but I have no such resonating story to tell in my own life.

I have experienced a transforming encounter with Christ, in my early twenties, but in the normal context of gospel preaching and opportunity for response. Since then the Bible, the Sacraments and relationships with fellow Christians have sustained me, but with no paranormal experience on the way.

Our son died in February at the age of 45, and his long and desperate struggle with cancer (without faith in Christ) has been an unsought but immense stretching of our faith (my wife and I) which we cannot compare with anything else we have suffered. I believe that had we been a couple less articulate, less inclined to receive from reading (especially the Scriptures), we might well have been supported by visionary experiences of Christ. This is not a complaint! We could not have been given more strength than we have received, frequently agonizingly, but without visions. I don't know whether all this is helpful to you. Forgive me if it is not.

There is so much in that letter of pain, of outreach, of concern for others, and of accepting the reality of other people's experiences which may differ from one's own, that one cannot append an adequate comment to it. But it does highlight the point that cultural diversity has an important bearing on our relationship with Jesus and that the way he approaches us is of his choosing, not ours. It is as though Jesus accommodates the way he approaches us to our personal and cultural situations.

The question the bishop raises about education is answered in part by Wiebe, who provided details of the scholastic levels attained by the 17 women and 11 men he had interviewed about their visionary experiences. All had attended high school, though three may not have stayed the course as they were categorized in a group labelled 'some high school'. Four had a university degree and another four had attended university, possibly without completing the degree course. Seven had made a specific study of theology. Of the 17 women, nine were primarily homemakers, one was a minister and there was an office manager, a nurse and library assistants. The men included a stockbroker, a retired teacher, an evangelist, five ministers and a labourer. [5] It follows that higher education is not a bar to visionary experiences but it may be associated with a reduced incidence of such experiences compared to those with a less sophisticated lifestyle. It is difficult to be certain about this. Six of the bishops who replied to my questionnaire indicated that they had had a clear perception of the risen Jesus similar to that recorded in the Gospels; though one crossed out the words: 'similar to that listed by Paul in 1 Corinthians 15: 3-8 and recorded in the Gospels.'

Some correspondents suggested that people's cultural heritage would affect any vision they may have, and this is a reasonable expectation. The following comments are indicative.

**Bishop 7.**

Visions of the Risen Christ must be presumably conditioned by previous expectations as to what he might look like, mostly drawn from the history of Christian art. After all, we have no actual historical picture. I wonder if any research has been done among other ethnic groups given the exciting new portrayals of Christ in African and Asian art, which contrast so much with our images of a Christ as a long-haired bearded Englishman.

**Bishop 8.**

I do find it difficult to understand how anyone can claim with complete certainty, centuries after the Resurrection, to recognize the face of Jesus, or to see Him in person as a human figure. The disciples may well have done at the Resurrection as they knew his face. It is not clear when Paul refers to the 'appearance' of Jesus to him that he was speaking of a visible sighting. We have no information in our time as to what Jesus actually looked like. For our ideas of his appearance we are dependent entirely on the works of artists, mostly European. And if we turn to Asian and African artists we get a very different facial picture, with different colour skin and different clothing.

The bishops' comments are relevant. We need to be aware of cultural differences and any tendency to stereotype our perception of Jesus. We need to remember that he was not a white European but from the Middle East and that his skin would have been dark and his eyes brown. But cultural stereotypes are not always inappropriate, and just as it is proper for European artists to depict Jesus as a white man, it is equally proper for people of other races to portray him as one of themselves. In fact, it is apparent from the bishops' comments that Christ is portrayed in African and Asian art in ways to which indigenous people can relate.

Wiebe listed the nationality of the people he interviewed. In his group of 28 people, there were 16 Canadians, eight Americans, two Australians, one Anglo-Irish and one Welsh. Their ethnicity is not given but it seems likely that most would have a European background. I know of no study within the Asian, African or Afro-Caribbean communities which has attempted to determine the incidence and nature of any visions those peoples may have had of Christ. The only study that I know along these lines was reported by Osis and Haraldsson in 1977. They undertook a cross-cultural survey of deathbed experiences that was based on reports provided by physicians and nurses in India and the USA (discussed in Chapter 7). Crucially, the study showed that while Christians may report seeing Jesus at the moment of death, the perceptions of Hindus are culturally different. It is perhaps relevant to say here that, from the studies on bereavement that are discussed in Chapter 9, we know that the incidence of visionary experiences recorded among widowed people does not differ with race, educational status, age or gender.

## Responses to questionnaire

In the questionnaire the bishops were asked to indicate whether or not they agreed with the following questions:

1. We know that 'we live and move and have our being in Him'. Apart from this, do you feel that the Holy Spirit is helping and guiding you in a discernible way?

Yes [ ]      No [ ]

2. We meet Jesus in a special way in the Sacraments. Apart from this, do you ever feel that Jesus as distinct from the Holy Spirit is with you, perhaps in a way that is difficult to describe in words?

Yes [ ]      No [ ]

3. Have you ever had a clear perception of the risen Jesus, similar to that listed by Paul in 1 Corinthians 15: 3-8 and recorded in the Gospels?

Yes [ ]      No [ ]

One bishop replied 'No' to all three questions.

Six bishops gave a positive response to all three questions and all six provided additional information in a covering letter or note. One asked that this additional information should be treated as 'strictly confidential please'. Consequently, I cannot give details of his most interesting response in this book. All six included their names.

Nineteen bishops replied 'Yes' to question 1 and 'No' to questions 2 and 3. Of these, ten sent an explanatory letter or covering note. Eleven bishops in this group withheld their names.

Thirty-two bishops replied 'Yes' to questions 1 and 2, and 'No' to question 3. Of these, twenty-four included a covering letter or explanatory note with the questionnaire. Among these, only ten chose to be anonymous.

Nine replies were more miscellaneous in content. Four bishops did not return the questionnaire, choosing instead to write quite lengthy letters. The following comments taken from two of the letters indicate reasons given for this alternative choice.

**Bishop 9.**

Thank you for your letter and questionnaire. Rather than tick the boxes on the questionnaire, I thought it would be more consonant with how I experience things to write about the matters you raise.

**Bishop 10.**

I am not happy to fill in the questionnaire as you have laid it out because I do not think I am a person who has the gift of the sixth sense but I am quite certain there are many people who do have this gift but who are hesitant to talk about it.

Bishop 10 went on to say that he was fascinated by the people I had named who claimed to have seen Christ in some physical form, and that he knew Kenneth McAll (whose experience is discussed in Chapter 8) very well.

Three bishops returned questionnaires that had been completed only in part, but all nine responders in this group provided thoughtful comments or letters with their replies. Interestingly, these bishops all supplied their names and addresses, as did the one bishop who ticked all three 'No' boxes on the questionnaire.

It was clear from their replies to the questionnaire that the large majority of the bishops (n=58, 86.5%) felt that the Holy Spirit was helping and guiding them in a discernible way. Similarly, a significant number (n=38, 56.7%) felt that Jesus, as distinct from the Holy Spirit, was with them in a way that was difficult to describe in words. In reality these figures should probably be higher as they do not include the data given separately by bishops who did not complete the questionnaire. Most surprisingly, six bishops (8.9%) claimed to have had a clear perception of the risen Jesus similar to that recorded in the Acts of the Apostles and in the Gospels.

## The personality of the bishops

The possibility that a relationship might exist between the readiness of the bishops to identify themselves and their responses to the questionnaire was examined, and it appears that such a relationship exists with question 2. When replies to the questionnaires were scrutinized, it was noted that bishops who provided a means of identification seemed more likely to experience the presence of Jesus than those who chose to remain anonymous. This possible association was examined using a Chi-squared test. Sixty bishops returned completed questionnaires and 40 answered 'Yes' to question 2 while 20 bishops said 'No'. Of the 40 bishops who answered 'Yes', 32 provided a means of identification, *viz.* their address and/or name. Of those who answered 'No', only nine were identifiable. The difference is statistically significant (Chi-squared = 7-46, $p < 0.05$). One cannot place much importance on this finding, particularly as the figures were obtained before the hypothesis was formulated, but it is interesting and may point to a basic psychological difference between the two groups of responders. This possibility might be of interest to future researchers.

It would have been helpful to have known the theological orientation of the responders. This would have enabled other hypotheses to be tested, such as: Does the likelihood of people experiencing the presence of Jesus vary with Churchmanship? Does the incidence differ between charismatic Christians and those more disposed to contemplative prayer? If so, are such variations open to theological, psychological or sociological explanations? And what about gender? Women were the first to witness the presence of the risen Jesus, and of the 28 case studies reported by Wiebe, 17 involved women while only 11 involved men. Will this difference be substantiated in any future study?

## Difficulties with the questionnaire

The difficulty bishops had with the questionnaire has been mentioned already. One bishop who first contacted me by e-mail, as he wished to discuss its implications with friends before replying, encountered such problems. He set out the result of their deliberations in the following letter. (A *caveat* is needed here. It may help to look at Appendix 3 before reading the letter.)

**Bishop 11.**

You will remember that we exchanged e-mails after I received your letter of July 21. We have now discussed it in a small group of thoughtful Christian people and I have these responses to make to your questionnaire. It is not easy to give a simple yes or no answer to any of the questions. Every member of the group was able to tell us of experiences which confirmed beyond doubt their faith in the risen Lord and His loving concern for them, but none was of a kind which could properly be set alongside the Resurrection appearances of Jesus as listed by St Paul in 1 Corinthians 15. We did not warm to the idea of a vision, or the use of the word 'sight' to describe our awareness. Even to speak of a 'clear perception' seemed too strong a term.

Everyone in our group found it impossible to distinguish between Jesus and the Holy Spirit in our experiences. I think Paul had a similar difficulty – for example in Acts 16: 6-10. In your second question, we do not know how we could feel the guiding of Jesus as distinct from the Holy Spirit. There was awareness that the sense of the guiding of God in our lives was real, although our awareness of it was more often seen in retrospect than at the moment of its happening

I served under Donald Coggan for four years as one of his Suffragan Bishops, and with Cuthbert Bardsley for a time on the Church Army Board, and I respect them both. But I find it very hard to credit Cuthbert's assertion that he had seen Christ as in 'an objective physical manner'. Surely this must have been a very personal and subjective experience. How did he recognise that this was 'the beloved face of our Lord'? Who knows what He looked like?

In a similar way we took issue with the account of Donald English that Jesus remained in the room for 3-4 minutes before walking out through the door. We can welcome and respond to an awareness of the presence of the Lord, but we cannot accept that He might come and walk among us in the same way that He did in the unique period between the Resurrection and the Ascension.

I don't know whether this is at all helpful, but thank you for providing the material for a very interesting discussion.

With all good wishes.

In reply, I wrote:

Dear Bishop,

Thank you very much for your thoughtful and most helpful letter. You rightly doubt Cuthbert's use of the term an 'objective physical manner' and I must admit they are my words not his. It is the interpretation I gave to his account of seeing Dorothy Kerin supported by Our Lord during a healing service at All Saints Parish Church, Leamington Spa a few months before she died.

He wrote that he was very concerned for her and as she was ascending the pulpit he prayed for her to be strengthened. He went on to say: 'Then a remarkable thing happened. Over Dorothy's face gradually appeared the face of Christ, until it was quite clear. For a few moments the beloved face of Our Lord was there, and then gradually faded away. I had clearly been shown that Christ was already there to strengthen her, and she carried on bravely to the end of the service.' [7]

The book is progressing quite well. I have completed Chapter 1 and started Chapters 2 and 3, but I am determined not to rush it. The response of the bishops has been marvellous; over 70% have replied and most have offered useful comments and/or accounts of personal experiences that they consider relevant. The sense of goodwill that I am receiving is immense.

Thank you very much for your help.

Yours sincerely

Bishop Cuthbert's perception of Christ at All Saints Church was clearly visionary. In that sense it is not comparable to the Resurrection experiences of the Apostles. But his growing awareness that Christ was present at the service can remind us of Jesus' approach to his followers at the Resurrection, and the way he enabled people to come to terms with his Resurrection gradually. The time lapse between his appearance and people's recognition of him varied; it was relatively short in the Garden but much longer on the road to Emmaus. On the road to Damascus, Saul still had to ask the question: 'Who are you, Lord?' before he knew for certain that he was confronted by Jesus of Nazareth. It is a problem that continues to face people who find themselves in the presence of the Holy One and yet, as the next letter reveals, it can be answered with assurance. This final letter covers a number of points which may usefully be included as a summation of the experiences and beliefs of many Christian people. It is written as a series of brief statements.

### Bishop 12.

I hope that this is helpful. My relationship with God is based on the truth that Jesus was raised from the dead.

* I find it hard to distinguish the different persons of the Trinity in my experience and relationship with God. There are times when I am aware of the presence of Jesus, but I am also aware then of the presence and activity of the Holy Spirit.

* I am convinced of the physical Resurrection of Jesus from the dead.

* In his Resurrection appearances to his followers (in New Testament times), Jesus was recognised, though not always immediately. I do not doubt those appearances – indeed, I am convinced of them – but there is an element of mystery here.

* I see Jesus as God incarnate, and I believe that God (Father, Son and Holy Spirit) makes himself known to me in ways I can grasp and understand.

* I believe that God has spoken to me at various points in my life. In particular he spoke to me one night when at the age of 17 I was seriously ill with tuberculosis. I cannot say whether it was a particular person of the Trinity.

* I have been aware that I have been in the presence of God on many occasions, but I have never seen Jesus.

* I have experienced the power of God in my life, and I am convinced that it is the power which raised Jesus from the dead.

* As I get older I am finding it increasingly impossible to separate the functions of the Holy Trinity. I am content to wait for the mystery to be revealed in Heaven!

Is this what you are looking for?

With best wishes.


## Comment/Summary

A postal questionnaire asking about their experiences of the risen Jesus was sent to 82 retired Anglican bishops resident in England. Sixty seven replied, a response rate of 81.7 per cent. This high response points to the innate courtesy of the bishops but it may also reflect the importance they gave to the study. The bishops were all men. They were all below the age 85 but it is possible that some non-responders were too ill to reply. The bishops did not just answer the three questions posed; some added short comments, others wrote lengthy letters, and a few asked specific questions – for instance, whether visions of Jesus might be influenced by education or cultural differences and if any research had been done in these areas.

One hypothesis tested a possible link between the bishops' personalities and the likelihood of their having had a close experience of Jesus. Little importance can be given to the finding at present, but it is interesting that bishops who could be identified (by name or address) when they returned the questionnaire were more likely to have experienced the presence of Jesus than those who remained anonymous. Of greater interest is the finding that five bishops stated unequivocally in the questionnaire that they had had an experience of Jesus similar to that recorded in the Gospels and by Paul in 1 Corinthians 15: 3–8.

# CHAPTER 5

# Bishops' Replies

WE SAW IN THE previous chapter that the large majority (86.5%) of the bishops felt that the Holy Spirit was helping and guiding them in a discernible way, and that most (56.7%) also felt that Jesus, as distinct from the Holy Spirit, was with them in a way that is difficult to describe in words. This chapter examines in greater detail the replies given to the questionnaire (see Appendix 4) by the bishops. Some repetition of the views they expressed is to be expected for two reasons. Firstly, because the bishops hold to a common belief in the nature and reality of the Trinity even though they may differ on other points of doctrine. Secondly, because in some instances it is appropriate to use short extracts from the bishops' letters more than once. In quoting from the letters, the bishops' individual styles are retained as closely as possible; thus any words they underlined or capitalised are maintained as in the original.

## The Trinity

Christianity is a Trinitarian faith. It asserts a belief in a triune God – Father, Son and Holy Spirit – co-eternal and co-equal. The three persons of the Trinity are also considered to be inter-dwelling and interdependent, a state that theologians call a 'circumincession'. As a consequence, and as John's Gospel and Paul make clear, there can be no experience of, faith in, or knowledge of Jesus except through the work of the Spirit; and the Spirit does nothing but witness to Jesus and the Father's will and presence within us and the world.

It is not surprising, therefore, that some correspondents had difficulty in distinguishing their experiences of Jesus from those of the Holy Spirit. When the questionnaire was being devised, it seemed likely that this problem would arise, but because I wanted to determine the extent to which senior members of the church believed that they had had experiences of the risen Jesus similar to those recorded in the Gospels, that specific question needed to be asked. Not surprisingly, some bishops wrote of their inability to differentiate between members of the Trinity in their replies. The essential Unity of the Trinity and the problems associated with attempts to distinguish between the Three Persons was mentioned by at least five responders. The following letters show this and point to the bishops' own experiences and opinions. We start with brief remarks from three bishops and conclude this section with two longer letters.

**Bishop 1.**

I find it hard to distinguish between different persons of the Trinity in my experience and relationship with God. There are times when I am aware of the presence of Jesus but I am also aware then of the presence and activity of the Holy Spirit.

**Bishop 2.**

It is natural for a Christian to speak of the presence of Jesus, but we need also to remember that it is part of our belief that we simply cannot distinguish, post Resurrection, between Jesus, the Holy Spirit and the Father. Jesus told us that He came to earth so that we may know and experience God the Holy Spirit.

**Bishop 3.**

As I get older I am finding it increasingly impossible to separate the functions of the Holy Trinity. I am content for the mystery to be revealed in heaven!

**Bishop 4.**

Thank you for your interesting letter of July 21. I find it difficult to answer your questions in a yes/no fashion, for the same, or at any rate similar reasons, as those for which I find it impossible to jump into EITHER the 'objective' or OK the 'subjective' box when asked to say what I believe about the presence of the risen Christ as attested in the New Testament.

I believe that Jesus was present to the apostles (i.e. they didn't dream it up or autosuggestion) but it was a presence (like that of Christ in the Eucharist) which can be apprehended only by faith, 'he who has eyes to see, let him see.'

I'm not sure what you mean by the possibility of apprehending the presence of Christ as distinct from that of the Holy Spirit. There is an old theological principle: opera trinitatis indivisa ad extra. In other words, as far as creation is concerned, the actions of the persons of the Holy Trinity are indivisible. To which you may want to answer: what then do we mean when we say that we pray in the Spirit through the Son to the Father. Have you written to Bishop Montefiore who I believe had a strong experience of the risen Lord when he became a Christian in his teenage years?

Yours sincerely

Author's comment  Providing a coherent answer to the question 'what do we mean when we pray in the Spirit through the Son to the Father?' is not easy, and I can best respond by asking another question: 'What did Jesus mean when he spoke in separate terms of the Father and of the Holy Spirit?' A possible reply to the question may be found in the next letter.

**Bishop 5.**

Thank you for your letter and questionnaire. Rather than tick the boxes on the questionnaire I thought it would be more consonant with how I experience things to write about the matters you raise.

You rightly quote from St Paul's words to the Court of Areopagus when he pointed out that the God he worshipped was closer than breathing and in everything he encountered because He was the creator of all that is and He sustains it constantly. For me those words are true to my experience. I can't say that I am consciously expecting that the Holy Spirit will help or point the way in discernible signs but I do believe that His sustaining and guiding care is surely and constantly around me, moving and working in the whole depth and breadth of my life and circumstances. Then from time to time there is the surprise of a sure sense that things have come together with the sure signs of His mark on them.

Your second question draws a distinction between Jesus and the Holy Spirit with the implication that we can experience them in different ways. I find that difficult to square with my experience. The Holy Spirit is the source of the miracle whereby Jesus the historical figure becomes for me a living presence and source of new life. The Holy Spirit does not have an independent ministry over and above the ministry of Jesus. Just as Jesus talks about being in the Father and the Father in Him so the Holy Spirit is in Jesus and Jesus in Him. The Holy Spirit sets us free to take on the likeness of Jesus.

Your third question asks whether I have shared the experiences of those who encountered Jesus in the immediate post-Resurrection days. On the Damascus road Paul did not see the configuration of Jesus' Resurrection body as the disciples saw Him on Easter Day and, of course, the disciples on the Emmaus road did not visually recognize the risen Christ when He walked with them. For me there have been moments when the presence of Jesus seemed sure even though there was no visual observation of Him. One such moment, for instance, was in 1962 at the Consecration Service in Coventry Cathedral as I stood beside Provost Howard in the Choir during the last hymn, 'O Worship the King'. Provost Howard turned to me and said, 'He's here!' and that was just what I too was thinking! No sight but nevertheless, certainty.

With my best wishes for the work you are undertaking.

Yours

## Replies to question 1

We know that 'we live, and move and have our being in Him'. Apart from this, do you feel that the Holy Spirit is helping and guiding you in a discernible way?

With two exceptions, all the bishops who completed the questionnaire answered 'Yes' to this question. Of the two exceptions, one replied 'No' to all three questions, whilst the other ticked 'Yes' to question 2 and 'No' to questions 1 and 3. Here are some of the additional comments that were received.

**Bishop 6.**

Yes. Usually through mental promptings or insights that have no other discernible origin.

**Bishop 7.**

Yes. But very occasionally, more when looking back.

**Bishop 8.**

Yes. But only in retrospect.

**Bishop 9.**

Yes. In my ministry I have been much aware of the presence of the Holy Spirit, however described, rather than Jesus the man.

**Bishop 10.**

Yes. I believe in a living God with whom I have contact in my prayers. As with all Christians it comes as no surprise, therefore, that I am conscious of His presence and aware of Him helping me each day. Having said this, I have no experience similar to St Paul and many others, and it neither surprises nor dismays me. That He is there is as much a reality as to see Him.

**Bishop 11.**

Yes. I can't say that I am consciously expecting the Holy Spirit
will help or point the way in discernible signs but I do believe that
His sustaining and guiding care is surely and constantly around me,
moving and guiding in the whole depth and breadth of my life and
circumstances. Then from time to time there is the surprise of a sure
sense that things have come together with the sure signs of His mark
upon them.

**Bishop 12.**

My conscious awareness of the guidance of the Holy Spirit has
been most poignant at the crucial times of decisions in my life over
marriage and the moves between Ministry. I take this to be the work
of the Holy Spirit. But in prayer if I have a picture in my mind it is
of speaking with the Lord Jesus.

**Bishop 13.**

It depends on what is meant by discernible – I have been conscious
inwardly that certain things had to be done and certain decisions to
be made.

## Comment

Almost without exception, all the bishops have a sense of being
helped and guided by the Holy Spirit. For some this support was
not perceived at the time it was given, but was appreciated later in
retrospect. Some bishops sensed it only at crucial moments of their
ministry, whilst others had a more constant awareness of the Holy
Spirit's presence. Though often sure of being guided and helped,
distinguishing the source of that help from within the Trinity can
be perplexing. The following examples are indicative.

### Bishop 14.

This bishop replied 'Yes' to question 1, indicating that he felt helped by the Holy Spirit, and 'No' to questions 2 and 3. Then he appended the following comment: 'I have had many experiences of an overwhelming sense of the Presence of Jesus in varied circumstances, but nothing could be interpreted as a physical representation.'

## Replies to question 2

We meet Jesus in a special way in the Sacraments. Apart from this, do you ever feel that Jesus as distinct from the Holy Spirit is with you, perhaps in a way that is difficult to describe in words?

Forty bishops answered 'Yes' to this question. Their comments will be discussed under five headings:

1) Worship

2) Prayer

3) Pastoral Care

4) Crucial Moments

5) Other people's experiences.

However, we start with two replies that do not fit into any of those categories.

### Bishop 15.

Yes. I have not had the kind of experience myself which you ask. I believe the risen Lord walks with me through every day, and will raise me from death to be with Him. I describe this as a spiritual experience.

### Bishop 16.

He replied 'Yes' to questions 1 and 2, then added: 'But since it is the work of the Holy Spirit to glorify Jesus, the distinctions may not be valid.'

## Worship

**Bishop 17.**

Often in worship.

**Bishop 18.**

With his people at worship.

**Bishop 19.**

Yes, as a companion and friend and often in worship.

**Bishop 20.**

Perhaps the most frequent experience is that of the presence of God in the midst of His people at worship. This would not always be so Christ-shaped though I would want to say that in God there is no un-Christ-Likeness.

**Bishop 21.**

I have never had a clear-cut vision of a 'physical' Christ, but over the years I have experienced, only on a number of occasions, a very strong spiritual awareness of His presence. This has sometimes been during the Eucharist but also sometimes at quite unexpected moments and occasionally in the shape of another human person – if that makes sense.

## Comment

The bishops often feel closest to Christ in prayer and worship. A memorable example of this was given earlier by Bishop 5 where he recalls how he was standing alongside Provost Howard during the Consecration Service in Coventry Cathedral and the Provost turned to him during the last hymn and said, 'He's here!' – expressing in those two words the bishop's own certainty of Christ's presence. Eleven bishops made similar unprompted comments.

## Prayer

### Bishop 22.

I converse with him regularly.

### Bishop 23.

Yes, in spirit.

### Bishop 24.

Yes, but since it is the work of the Holy Spirit to glorify Jesus the distinction may not be valid..

### Bishop 25.

Question 2 comes nearest to a 'sense of awareness' from time to time but especially, but not only in prayer.

### Bishop 26.

In prayer if I have a picture in mind it is of speaking with the Lord Jesus.

## Pastoral care

### Bishop 27.

Some of the most powerful experiences have arisen from Ignatian contemplation when it has been clear that we have talked together. I am also very clear that I have met Jesus in some personal pastoral visiting. In so many parochial visits I received more than I gave – often in being with individuals of little education or status in the world. As a Franciscan tertiary, I see these moments rather like Francis with the leper – a meeting with Jesus.

### Bishop 28.

With regard to your second request I don't have much to contribute.

I cannot pretend to any visible manifestations of the Risen Christ. However spiritual experiences have often been 'Christ-Shaped' rather than vaguely numinous. On my way to mission work in South America, a conversation with a Mexican carpenter in a bus brought a wonderful awareness of the presence of the carpenter of Nazareth. I have appreciated the Ignatian 'incarnational' approach after doing the Exercises. However perhaps the most frequent experience is that of the presence of God in the midst of people at worship.

**Bishop 29.**

I have no experience of the kind that Donald English and Cuthbert Bardsley recount. However a sense of the presence of the risen Christ has been my privilege on a number of occasions in pastoral situations both in this country and during my 20 years of ministry in East Africa.

(a) At the side of the wife of the first Christian convert in the Samburu tribe killed as the result of the crazy driving of the young son of a chief, such a tragic loss to the Christian community (1959).

(b) Watching a young Kikuyu Christian get out of his seat and cross the floor of the grass hut in which we were having a mug of tea; he then embraced the man who had just entered; he had last seen him ten years previously when the man had left him dying of machete wounds because he wouldn't take the oath (to kill whites). He embraced him with tears as he forgave him and they were reconciled. His name was Erastus; he was our driver. There are other occasions both abroad and here but they are not so dramatic.

## Crucial moments

Jesus said, 'Ask and you will receive, seek and you will find, knock and the door will be opened to you,' so it comes as no surprise that moments of crisis bring an increased sense of support, if one asks for it. This is my own experience but the asking has always involved seeking the strength and/or ability to do something for someone else. The bishops have provided the following examples.

**Bishop 30.**

There have been about half a dozen times when I have felt clear and
definite presence and guidance. For the rest it seems that my calling
is to bumble along as fruitfully and prayerfully as I can.

**Bishop 31.**

At a time of considerable anxiety and stress I experienced a feeling
of complete tranquillity and peace, as a result of repeating His name,
'Jesus,' a number of times. Though I have repeated the exercise from
time to time, the same experience has not resulted.

**Bishop 32.**

I cannot say that I have had Cuthbert Bardsley's experience, but I
have had many strong experiences in the same order over the years.
They may not be of help to you in writing your book but I set them
down for you by way of interest.

In 1940 I was a 15 year old away at school in Northallerton. On
Michaelmas day I had cycled over to Ripon with friends. They
went to explore places and I went to the Cathedral where I knew
the assistant organist; in fact he was my organ tutor. Someone was
playing the organ and I sat quietly in the nave. The music was
moulded by the architecture of the building and my sensitivities
were heightened by this. It was at a time when I was wondering
what to do with my life – music or the navy. In the 'quietness' I was
suddenly aware of a presence. It was as though hands were extended
to me and my inclination was to reach out and take them with
my hands. It was a very powerful moment for a fifteen year old. I
couldn't talk about it – not even to the school chaplain who was a
close friend. But it was something that I treasured.

In 1946 I was detached from my regiment having fought our
way up through Holland to Germany, and was admin officer of
8 Corps Church House. This was an establishment set up by the
Army Chaplain's department, to prepare soldiers of all ranks for
demob, and especially men who might be ordinands in any of the
denominations. We had taken over an *adeligen* [sic] community
together with their huge Priory Church, library and residential
houses. This was where I first met with some of the 'names' of the
day including Cuthbert Bardsley.

Our DACG (Deputy Assistant Chaplain General) was Philip Wheeldon, later Bishop of Kimberley and Kuruman, and his office was in Church House. Philip encouraged me along with many others to test my vocation to the ministry. He became my director and encouraged me to keep a 'nightly watch' in one of the chapels. It was here that my Ripon experience happened many times again. In fact it was more specific and the presence was a person. Again the hands were significant though I could not discern the face. However the sense of meeting was very humbling and formative, and changed my whole approach to the work I was doing.

In 1955, during a period of difficulty about my future, I happened to be in Datchet Church for a clergy quiet day. During the lunch period I stayed in the church. Again I had this strong sense of presence with hands outstretched. I accepted that this was an invitation to be led on to the next stage of what God wanted me to do. It was remarkable that Philip Wheeldon, who was then Cyril Garbett's Chaplain at Bishopthorpe, came down shortly after this to say that Garbett wanted me to come back to Yorkshire and to take on a difficult assignment in Middlesbrough.

Experiences of this order, very personal with a strong sense of Presence and sometimes Person, have happened to me throughout my ministry. They have not been limited to periods of uncertainty – though they have been strong at such times. Rather they have occurred unexpectedly. They are as vivid as ever and I have come to see them as moments when my ministry at that time is validated and supported. This may be a bit off the track you are exploring but if it is of any help to you I am glad.

## Other People's Experiences

Some bishops wrote of being told by other people of occasions when they were aware that Jesus was with them.

### Bishop 33.

During my time as Bishop of…I developed a link between the diocese and the Evangelical Lutheran Church in Latvia. During two visits to Latvia we met a number of young Pastors and others who had recently come to Faith. In the Churches we found a whole generation missing who had been brought up in an atheistic philosophy. One such young Pastor was Injus Daukts. He had done service in the Russian navy and was a student exploring the Faith. He had read the Bible. On the day there was the famous human line of people from Tallinn (in Estonia) to Vilnius (in Lithuania) he found himself on the line at Riga facing the Russian guns. He knew the Risen Lord to be beside him and he heard a voice saying, 'I am the Resurrection and the Life.' In that moment he knew his mortality and today is Pastor in one of the churches in Riga. He had no doubt the Lord had appeared to him.

**Bishop 34.**

I describe in my book *The Christian Healing Ministry* [2] how I was called to the bedside of our verger, very seriously ill with cancer in hospital, the doctor saying he would not last the night. I anointed him with difficulty (he was in an oxygen tent) with the curtains drawn round the bed – it was about midnight, the nurse and my wife being with me. A rough Yorkshire man called me over to his bed opposite and said, 'Summat's 'appened behind them curtains!' In the morning the doctors found his blood count to be normal and the sister remarked, 'What happened? The language has cleared up!' He was back at work in a fortnight and gave a wonderful witness to his healing by Christ. He died of the disease 2 years later, but glowed for those 2 years. The Yorkshire man was right. The risen Christ was present and raised him up. It was a great encouragement to the parish's healing work, and mine.

I was interested in all you said. I followed Cuthbert Bardsley as Bishop Visitor to Burrswood and lived there for four years while I was Advisor on Healing to both Archbishops. During this time I listened to Dorothy Kerin's confessions and wrote a book *The Vision of Dorothy Kerin,* now sadly out of print – Burrswood should have copies: address is 'Groombridge' near Tunbridge Wells, TN3 9PY. Personally I have always felt a strong faith in the Risen Christ, alive today, and also the exquisite joy of the Easter Festival. I have experienced Resurrection in my life.

PS. Dorothy Kerin saw the risen Christ and was frequently aware of His Presence. She also saw Our Lady. Her Church is 'Christ the Healer'.

PPS. All the best for your book.

## Replies to question 3

Have you ever had a clear perception of the risen Jesus, similar to that listed by Paul in 1 Corinthians 15: 3-8 and recorded in the Gospels?

Six bishops answered 'Yes' to question 3 – an unexpectedly high response rate to that particular question. Two bishops indicated the nature of the events they experienced, but most were reluctant to give much more information. This reluctance is understandable, as it is always difficult to reveal in detail one's most cherished experiences, particularly if such experiences might become public property. The following comments and letters are illustrative. Some are quite short comments which were written on the questionnaire.

Bishop 35. This bishop ticked 'Yes' in all three boxes but in question 3 crossed out the words: 'similar to that listed by Paul in 1 Corinthians 15: 3-8 and recorded in the Gospels.' He wrote:

> I respond to your questionnaire. I don't like to talk about it but I have written about my conversion experience in seeing the risen Lord in my autobiography O God What Next? (Hodder 1995, pp1-3). I am not sure if it was the same as in 1 Corinthians 15: 3-8 because I don't know how they saw him. I wrote the blurb for Wiebe's Canadian edition of Visions of Jesus, where the visions (as all visions) include a subjective component. I have Healing the Family Tree but it hardly bears on this subject. I have a whole chapter on visions in my The Paranormal – A Bishop Investigates by Upfront Publishers and available from Avalon. I include it in my views about the Resurrection as a 'veridical hallucination' used by the risen Lord as a means of communication, including a subjective factor (e.g.) we always see Jesus clothed despite the grave clothes found in the empty tomb. With best wishes for your enterprise.

Bishop 36. This response was brief. Alongside question 2 he wrote, 'Yes, in the Spirit,' and by question 3: 'Yes, at most not quite so physically *visible* as in Paul and the Gospels.' He included a most interesting letter about his experiences but its contents cannot be disclosed as the bishop headed the letter: 'Strictly *Confidential Please.*'

Bishop 37. He gave no answer to question 2 but he did add this comment: 'I cannot distinguish between the presence of Jesus with the presence at work of the Holy Spirit.' He answered 'Yes' to question 3 and wrote: 'But how clear was the appearance to Paul? He does not tell us, and we must not assume we can know how Paul received the Resurrection. We live in a very different culture.'

Bishop 38. He answered 'Yes' to all three questions and added: 'I thank you for the work you are doing on this important nay vital subject.' Nothing else was written but I wonder what experiences had elicited such a positive remark.

Bishop 39. This bishop answered 'Yes' to all three questions but gave no data about his experiences. However, he did add the following comment: 'I wish the Church in the West could rediscover the reality of the presence of the Holy Spirit in all aspects of life.'

Bishop 40. This bishop answered 'Yes' to questions 1 and 3 but 'No' to question 2. He wrote: 'You must forgive me for not writing as to your second query. I am very old now and looking forward to myself being caught up in the spirit – Spirit of God, Spirit of Christ – I can get as excited as Paul about all this, because without wishing to set out definitions, I believe strongly in the Resurrection to eternal life. My favourite Resurrection story is the Feeding of the Five Thousand – the broken fragments are collected 'so that nothing is lost'. And that I believe is what God in Christ and Christ in God does to each of us, in the power of the Holy Spirit.

## 'No' to question 3

Most bishops answered 'No' to this question. That is to be expected. Christians do not expect to see Jesus in his bodily form and the recorded instances of such happenings are few. However, people do experience the Risen Christ in other ways and it is apparent from their responses that some bishops experience a relationship with Jesus in ways that have not been mentioned already. The following responses are illustrative.

Bishop 41. No, but the time I said 'Lord, here am I, send me' on my knees in response to God's call, the rooms seemed blazing with light even though it was 1 a.m.

Bishop 42. There is often deep consciousness of the Risen Christ coming to take his child home at the time of death – very moving to be there.

Bishop 43. There have been many other Special moments when I have been overwhelmed by Christ acting when things were impossible – and reassuring with words to my mind or a hug like a blanket.

Bishop 44. I cannot claim to have an extra-normal experience of Jesus. I do have very vivid feeling of the omnipresence of God in creation and in a special way in the Church. That is what Jesus told us to expect in the Gospel of John. Whether or not those were our Lord's *ipsissima* words, it is completely consistent with the early days of the Church.

Bishop 45. I do not doubt for one moment the possibility of his appearing to Christians and am prepared to give credence to the testimonies of those who have described such occurrences. I have never had the joy, but recognize that they are simply instances of his grace to people who possibly had great need of the assurance of his presence at certain points in their lives.

Bishop 46. Thank you for your letter. I attach the questionnaire, completed as far as I can. I can understand, and have myself experienced the presence of the Holy around and within me. It is natural for a Christian to speak of the presence of Jesus, but we need also remember that it is part of our belief that we cannot simply distinguish post-Resurrection, between Jesus, the Holy Spirit and the Father. Jesus told us that he came to earth that we may know and experience God the Holy Spirit.

The Resurrection story is, I suggest, the best way that the early Christians could convey to those not present what a powerful, mysterious, wonderful event they had been privileged to witness. But they could only tell us of this tremendous experience in words. And words, useful, essential as they are, cannot convey the full meaning of what had happened and is happening. We must not think that clarity of verbal expression necessarily reveals all. This is the limitation of creeds and doctrines. They attempt to capture in words something so much deeper than any words can describe. We need to make the attempt but we must recognize and accept the limitations of trying to put belief about God into words. If we do not accept, for example, that, however fundamental to our Christian faith is the Gospel account of the Resurrection, yet it can only begin, because it is dependent on words, to show us the power and mystery of God at work at that time and today. If we do not remember this we shall belittle the majesty and the mystery of God.

## Attitudes to the Resurrection

The nature of Jesus' Resurrection has become one of the most controversial imponderables of Christian theology. Many believe that he rose from the dead in physical form, others that he appeared in a spiritual body, and some suggest that his appearance is best explained in more modernistic terms. For instance, can a belief in the physical Resurrection of Jesus be equated with some level of uncertainty about the nature of the physical body? One current hypothesis accepts the physicality of his Resurrection body but suggests that it was composed of a different substance from the one that was crucified. The underlying idea is that the Resurrection body was in truth a three-dimensional solid structure and not a spiritual body, that it was composed of a material that was not carbon based but one capable of producing a transformed and glorious body. Most bishops avoided such metaphysical uncertainties. However, they expressed varying views on the subject and these are offered under four headings:

1) He rose physically from the dead 2) Not dogmatic 3) Changed Lives 4) Less traditional views.

## He rose physically from the dead

Bishop 47. I certainly believe in the miracle of Jesus' Resurrection and in the historicity of the empty tomb, both because of the witness of Holy Scripture, the evidence of the early Church and the reality of the living Christ today, for which no other explanation is adequate.

Bishop 48. My own belief in the Resurrection is firmly based on the Gospel accounts of the empty tomb and the bodily appearances of our Lord to his disciples. Whilst I have no personal or second-hand experiences of the type you describe in your letter, I do not doubt their possibility. No-one could be a devotee of Julian of Norwich as I am without believing that such manifestations are within the bounds of faith possibility!

Bishop 49. My beliefs about the Resurrection are related to the fact that I believe in the bodily Resurrection from the grave of our Lord Jesus Christ and that he now lives and reigns in majesty at his Father's right hand. That belief is founded on the Scriptural evidence, the prophecies of the Old Testament and the promises of Jesus himself, and the fact of his appearances not only immediately after the Resurrection but also to Paul. I do not doubt for one moment the possibility of his appearance to Christians and am prepared to give credence to the testimony of those who have described such occurrences.

Bishop 50. I am convinced of the physical Resurrection of Jesus from the dead.

Bishop 51. I believe that Jesus rose physically from the dead, and that, for example, Thomas was able to put his finger in to the nail prints of His hands.

## Not dogmatic

Bishop 52. To me, belief in the Resurrection of Our Lord Jesus Christ is central to Christian belief. 'If Christ is not risen our Faith is vain.' I believe the tomb was empty but I am not dogmatic about the nature of the Resurrection Body which appeared between Easter and the Ascension. My Faith has been strengthened and encouraged by those who have had a conscious meeting with the Risen Lord.

Bishop 53. I do believe that the Risen Lord Jesus can/does appear to people in special times and circumstances (as to Donald English, Cuthbert Bardsley in your letter) but I cannot claim to have had such objective experiences myself.

## Changed Lives

Bishop 54. As far as my own belief in the Resurrection of our Lord is concerned, I grew up in a family which rarely went to church; my father was something of a sceptic, the result maybe of spending two years during World War I in the trenches. My own faith came to life when a school friend invited me to tea and then accompany him to a church service. I resisted the church bit, saying that I was not really interested in museums (!) but he assured me that the service to which he wanted to take me would not be like that. So I went. I was 17 years old, in the sixth form at Dulwich College. The following Easter Sunday evening service when the sermon was based on the Emmaus Road story so impressed me that I asked to be prepared for Confirmation and believed that I now had found Jesus to be real and that He is alive. However, I went up to Cambridge and shortly afterwards into the R.A.F. and my belief in the physical Resurrection of Jesus went through a four-year period of being a 'no go' area intellectually. I still believed that Jesus was alive but felt that I could not argue the cause of that item of the accepted historic creeds.

It was after I was released from the R.A.F. and instead of returning to Magdalene College went to the London School of Theology and read among other works, Fred Morrison's classic *Who Moved the Stone* and C.S. Lewis' *Miracles* that I came to a more personal belief in the Resurrection. However, after more than 50 years of ministry I find that evidence for the Resurrection rests far more on the incredible changes in the disciples and the growth of the early church than the evidence of the empty tomb – weighty though that circumstantial evidence is. I suppose if I were asked what most convinces me of the Resurrection it would have to be the totally changed direction of my life in my late teens and early twenties in view of my background.

## Less Traditional Views on the Resurrection

Bishop 55. Your views about the Resurrection is so huge a question that I certainly cannot attempt it in full in this letter. If you mean 'what happened at the Resurrection?' my view is what I take the Bible to say, namely that Jesus rose but did not return to his previous state. In this, Jesus differs from what happened presumably to Lazarus, and indeed the situations are completely different.

The Bible says that Jesus rose from death but then goes on to say that he appeared from time to time, usually unexpectedly, in a way which is inconsistent with someone merely returning to a former life. John makes the point that Jesus appeared to a group in hiding, and since John never wastes a word and is the latest of the Gospels to be written, I believe that we may take this as the considered view of someone present at some of the post-Resurrection events or, at least, someone who knew someone who was present at some of the post-Resurrection appearances. St. Paul's view – which you mention – is surely not a 'dead man walking' experience.

To put it briefly, I think we have here a true Resurrection which is the pioneering of a new form of life in creation as we know and understand it. This new life is available to all through the work of the Holy Spirit, but it was pioneered in and through Jesus by the work of God in one who was and is uniquely in communion with God, Father and Spirit. Jesus blazed the trail – as the writer to the Hebrews puts it – and we are invited to follow where he pioneered the way.

What happened at the tomb on Easter Day has always seemed to me to have the ring of truth about it as no-one who was organizing a persuasive story for 2,000 years ago would have written in that way. Firstly, the story is not hierarchical (think how the Vatican would have put Peter there first!), secondly it was a woman who met Jesus (in an age of even greater male arrogance than we have now), and thirdly there is the surprise of all concerned which is very evident. This is not the way a committee or PR consultant would have done it. Whether a camera would have been able to photograph the newly risen Jesus seems to me to be a cheap and silly question. It is the evidence of changed lives that argues for the eternal validity of the One who was raised. I hope your research goes well and, if you are able to reflect on why the Creeds say 'He rose again' and the Bible says 'He was raised', I shall be most interested because I find this discrepancy one of the most intriguing and 'hidden' questions in theology.

Bishop 56. I think I find it easier to believe in the Resurrection of all life, especially human life, rather than the bodily Resurrection of Jesus, but Jesus is a 'first fruit' – a sign to the rest of us of the reality of the Resurrection. But while we are each of us raised, we are raised as part of something much bigger than ourselves. My only experience is of a sense of at-oneness with all humanity and creation which recurs but I know someone in New Zealand who has experienced conversations with St. Stephen. His name is Michael Cocks and he has published a book called *The Stephen Experience*. He can be contacted on cocks@ihug.co.nz Although the account is rather incoherent I have found it has affected me deeply, especially my sense of life beyond death. The ISBN of the book is 0-959-79981-8.

Bishop 57. When asked to say what I believe about the presence of the risen Christ as attested in the New Testament, I believe that Jesus was present to the apostles (i.e. that they didn't dream it up, no auto-suggestion) but it was a presence (like that of Christ in the Eucharist) which can be apprehended only by faith.

Bishop 58. By contemporary ways of thinking, Jesus' Resurrection is inexplicable. I rely on (a) the witness testimony of the empty tomb (b) the concept that the Resurrection appearances are an inexplicable irruption from a different time/space dimension, unknown to most of us.

Bishop 59. I have never since the 60s been sure about the Empty Tomb and Bodily Resurrection as portrayed by the most traditional. But I have never doubted the experience of those who were present at the Resurrection appearances because I have found it quite impossible to deny that 'Jesus as distinct from the Holy Spirit is with me'. I have believed that even when at times I can't feel His Presence.

Bishop 60. Two issues may interest you. Firstly, when in hospital recovering from surgery I had, just prior to regaining proper consciousness, an awareness of all that was happening in the ward, and after two or three days of being heavily sedated, a clear vision of being supported by angels. With hindsight the angels looked just like traditional portrayals and I was strongly drugged. The vision was, nevertheless, hugely reassuring and therapeutic for me but I could not claim it as objective given my medical treatment.

(His second point, which considers the relationship that may exist between visions of Jesus and his portrayal in Christian art, is discussed in Chapter 4 under the heading 'Cultural Diversity'.)

## Final letters

Bishop 61. My relationship with God is based on the truth that Jesus was raised from the dead.

Bishop 62. This bishop did not provide a 'Yes/No' answer to question 3. Instead he wrote: 'I would respond to your main question by saying that I am not able to claim visionary experience of Jesus. However, my conviction is more in the 'hearing his voice' and 'sensing his presence' category. My own call to ministry is a case in point and when asked, 'Do you think that you are truly called according to the will of Our Lord Jesus Christ...' etc (BCP Ordination Question) I gladly still answer, 'I think so,' based on my first encounter with his 'voice' in 1950.'

The bishop did not divulge what the voice said to him but he obviously had had an experience that was meaningful to him and one that was to affect the subsequent course of his life. Other priests and ministers will have had similar experiences and it is likely that a large proportion would wish to respond 'Amen' to his declaration of belief.

## Comment/Summary

The questionnaire provided the bishops with an immediate problem. They were asked to distinguish between two persons of the Holy Trinity – the Son and the Holy Spirit – in their effect on the bishops' own lives. Not surprisingly, some respondents pointed out that, because the persons of the Holy Trinity are indivisible, this could not be done. On the other hand, others managed to do so. A large majority of the bishops (86.5%) believed that the Holy Spirit was helping and guiding them in a discernible way, and most (56.7 %) felt that Jesus, as distinct from the Holy Spirit, was with them in a way that is difficult to describe in words. In reply to question 3, which asked: 'Have you ever had a clear perception of the risen Jesus similar to that listed by Paul in 1 Corinthians 15: 3-8 and recorded in the Gospels?' five answered unequivocally 'Yes'. One other ticked the box but crossed out the words that referred to Paul and the Gospels.

Some bishops wrote of a strong sense of Presence and even of Person in their relationships with God. This tended to be most common during prayer and worship; for some it was particularly apparent at crucial moments of their life; for others it was most noticeable during pastoral visits where a chance encounter seemed sometimes like a meeting with Jesus himself.

The bishops were united in the importance they ascribed to the Resurrection but their views on the bodily nature of the risen Jesus varied considerably. This was not a subject that was posed in the questionnaire, but sixteen bishops offered comments – some at length and others briefly. Only four expressed a firm belief in the physical Resurrection of Jesus. Most seemed uncertain whilst others expressed quite radical views, including the suggestion that Jesus' Resurrection appearances are 'an inexplicable irruption from a different time/space dimension, unknown to most of us'. If this last view were true, it might help to explain the similarities that sometimes appear to exist between the pre-Ascension appearances of Christ and his appearing to people today.

# Section 3

# The Visions

# CHAPTER 6

# Meeting Jesus

E ACH PERSON'S SPIRITUAL JOURNEY is marked by moments of enlightenment that are intensely personal. In addition, there are experiences that we share in common with fellow Christians and even people of other faiths; for instance, an uplift in mood when we join together in worship. This can happen regardless of the form of worship or where it takes place. An awareness of the presence of the Holy One can be experienced in the quiet of a Quaker meeting, in the ritualised simplicity of the Eastern Orthodox liturgy, during an Evangelical Mission Praise meeting or at an inter-faith service. It is an aspect of the Christian life that we can share with many people throughout the world.

A less frequent happening is a direct encounter with Jesus of the sort recorded in the Gospels and the Acts of the Apostles. The Western Church has never encouraged the disclosure of such revelations; in fact it tends to discourage them, although the reasons for this are obscure. It is possibly because the early Fathers needed to ensure that the special nature and significance of Christ's Resurrection were not challenged when the Church was emerging during the first centuries of the Christian era. Whatever explanation we give or attitude we take, his Resurrection was a unique event and one of universal significance. But this does not mean that we should dismiss as insignificant those personal experiences that enable people to relate more closely to that revelation.

Every religion needs an established dogma that defines its

beliefs and practices. This is a source of strength, but taken to extremes it can create a structure of rigid intolerance that labels anyone who deviates, even slightly, from established doctrine as a heretic. The anchorite Dame Julian of Norwich (1342–1416) was fortunate to live in a relatively tolerant age when she wrote *Revelations of Divine Love*, the first book to be written in English by a woman. In it she speaks of the visions she had of Jesus and how they came to her. The revelations came, she said, in three distinct ways: by physical sight, by words formed in the intellect, and by spiritual sight. Of physical sight revelations, she said that she had tried to describe them 'as truthfully as I can'; of the words formed in her intellect that 'I had repeated them exactly as our Lord showed them to me'; and about the spiritual sight that 'I have said a fair amount but I can never describe it fully'. [1] This seems to be a primary problem with personal accounts of meetings with Christ: they can be so overwhelming that people find it is impossible to describe them precisely; or, as the Gospel accounts indicate, convince others of their reality. (More will be said of Julian's visions in Chapter 12.)

Of the people who wrote to me, Bishop Hugh Montefiore is among those who had an unforgettable meeting with Jesus early in life. He mentioned it in his letter but also more fully in his autobiography, *Oh My God, What Next?* Although not unique, it is an unusual story, the details of which are closer to those of St Paul's meeting with Jesus than to the accounts reported in the Gospels. The encounter happened in 1936 when Bishop Hugh – then a 16-year-old Jewish boy – was sitting alone in his study at Rugby School in central England. He was 'indulging in a pleasant adolescent gloom' when, suddenly, he became aware of a figure in white. It was not a solid figure but something that he perceived in his 'mind's eye' – yet he knew instinctively it was Jesus. [2] He heard the words 'Follow me' but he does not tell us whether he heard these words with the physical senses or, as

Julian of Norwich did, inwardly in the intellect. I think the latter form of communication is the more likely because people granted Christic visions often mention hearing an inner voice; and the auditory hallucinations that are associated with psychotic states, such as schizophrenia, are usually perceived as having a source outside the individual, rather than arising from within. Whatever the precise nature of the encounter may have been, the effect was dramatic. Bishop Montefiore said:

It was an indescribably rich event that filled me afterwards with overpowering joy. I could do no other than follow those instructions. I found that I had become a Christian as a result of a totally unexpected and most unusual spiritual experience, though that was not how I would have put it at the time. I was aware of the living Christ, and because of that I was aware of God in a new way. People ask me why and when I decided to convert. I did not decide at all; it was decided for me.

## Women of Coventry

The response of the Anglican bishops to my request for information was excellent. Within the diocese the clergy were less forthcoming, probably because my approach to them was more impersonal. No parish clergy contacted me but I had replies from three lay people – all of whom were women. All three asked for their names not to be disclosed. Of these, two were members of the Coventry Diocesan Cursillo and one was also a lay reader, a voluntary ministry that is unique to the Anglican Church. Established in 1866, the office of Reader is the only nationally accredited lay ministry that is governed by Canon Law and is episcopally licensed. Readers undertake many of the duties that were formerly the task of the parish priest, and its ministry attracts men and women from a wide range of backgrounds.

My three lay correspondents gave six separate accounts of

encounters with Jesus. Two letters have been edited; this was done partly to preserve the anonymity of the writers and partly for reasons of length. In choosing the extracts to print, I wanted the personality rather than the identity of the writer to emerge and still keep their accounts relevant to the theme of the book. The first correspondent wrote having seen my note in the Cathedral Newsletter (Appendix 1). The next two were members of Coventry Cursillo (Appendix 2).

## Letter 1

First of all, thank you for allowing me to write to you, to share a little of my spiritual journey. I will introduce myself, as I have not met you (as far as I know)...I grew up in a very intense Christian fellowship that lived and taught 'living in the world yet not of the world'. By the age of 14 years I was pushing at these boundaries longing to be set free, without ever really experiencing any Relationship with Jesus or God my Father...I became very fearful, even crying in school that 'I wouldn't be saved'. Hell was preached as a reality that each one of us needs to consider as the only alternative to a deep conviction of Salvation...I stayed away from the church and all Christian teaching for many years until I divorced at the age of 45 years. At this time my daughter became a Christian through Alpha and an Evangelical C of E church. I gradually began to visit churches – all Anglican, not to attend services, rather to sit quietly and often to light a candle.

After my first experience of an Alpha supper, I became very aware of the Presence of the Risen Lord. It stays with me until this day and is still very recent in my experience...I believe with all my heart that the Presence I met was the Risen Lord. His whole being was Light and white and he waited above the earth, not on the ground, yet in the room. I believe that He knew me from my early years' experiences, that I found the cross too painful to consider and Eternity as fearful as Hell. His being was larger than ours yet very real, not as a ghost or transient – yet most powerfully of all, was His Presence and His Voice.

Several times since, His Presence and person has been very close to me, always with words to guide and always with a reassurance that 'He will be with us until the end of the Age'... As I sat in the cathedral, in the chapel of Christ the Servant on Wednesday this week, I was very influenced by the sculptures 'Blind faith'. They spoke to me very much of our awakenings – spiritually between God and others. It was a very windy day yet as I sat listening to His voice, the wind and the organ music, I became less aware of seeking Him, rather becoming part of His Presence. To start with I had spoken quietly to one or two visitors – after 2 hours or more, I felt unable to speak at all. He was not there as Lord yet I was in His Presence. I was experiencing prayer in another way, feeling that this is to lead me to be in His Presence at all times.

## Comment

This first letter is more mystic in tone than those from the other correspondents who are quoted in this book and it has been heavily edited; but it does provide a useful insight into the type of experience that can occur and how this might lead into a more contemplative form of prayer and perhaps even union with God. I wonder too if she might have entered a trance-like state, as happened to Paul when he was praying in the temple and was told to leave Jerusalem and go to the Gentiles (Acts 22: 17–21).

## Letter 2

It was good to speak to you the other night, what follows are my three encounters with Jesus...My first encounter was right at the beginning of my Christian journey, before I made any formal commitment 10 years ago. I came to meet the Lord through the Bible – Ecclesiastes introduced me to Jesus! However, before I ever got into John's Gospel, every time I opened my Bible, the oddest things would happen – my head was suddenly filled with loud noise and the words would 'jump around' so I couldn't read them properly. This happened time after time until one day suddenly, there was the Lord! A tall figure, not solid, stood in the room and simply held up His right arm as if to give a blessing and said 'Peace', not audibly but straight into my being. A vision perhaps. All I know is, it was real because ever since that moment I was able to read my Scriptures and enjoy them and learn from them. In fact, since becoming a Christian, I've gone on to study with L.S.theol, achieved all 6 of their Bible studies and am on their 'leisure route' to a Diploma in Theology! Praise Him!

The second encounter happened a few years later when we lived in Salford. We as a family – I've one daughter – were having a very rare night out together. My ex-husband decided to take us out for an evening meal to a restaurant in the Peak District. It was early in the year, bitterly cold and very dark. When we were almost there, we hit ice on the road and the car started to career on the wrong side of the road, towards the bank. Suddenly, there on the right side of the road was the Lord – very brightly I might say! – as if 'pulling' the car towards Himself. He was there just for a moment; enough to bring the car to safety – I am convinced my ex-husband saw something because, back at the restaurant, he had a catharsis. He told me then of an affair he was having, and had been for a long time, with his P.A., although afterwards he could not recall a word he had said and had no recollection of this conversation.

Sometimes there are dates which remain in your memory because of the events of that day. One such date with me is 24th March 1996. By then, the marriage was all but dead. However, as a last ditch attempt to rescue it, we'd decided to visit a counsellor

– the meeting with her was an absolute disaster. In my heart I knew I was facing divorce. In my head I was panicking and desperately wanted to 'escape' from my ex-husband, who by then had added aggression to his list. Opposite our house was a spinney which I often walked through. This time, when I went in, there were two figures standing in front of me. I stopped and stared – they were not solid, but very real. On my left, a short stocky figure; an ugly little man carrying a heavy chain. On my right, My Lord, tall, and again very bright. I remember such an overriding feeling of love – almost of being cuddled – coming from Him that I walked in His direction. He was with me for a moment as we walked together and then He was gone. Maybe not really, as I'm sure He carried me for the next few years.

It has been very difficult writing these down, as this is the first time I've disclosed it. I hope they make sense. On the face of it they might seem crazy, which is probably why I've kept quiet about them until now. Again I would ask anonymity if you use any of these stories. Thanks. However, I know they happened and they were real. Jesus really does live! God bless.

## Letter 3

I know the writer of the next letter quite well. She was instrumental in my becoming a 'guide' at Coventry Cathedral and we would sometimes meet on Friday mornings at the Litany of Reconciliation which is held weekly in the ruins of the old Cathedral. I was completely unaware of her spiritual experiences before I read her letter. She begins with a few paragraphs that speak of her early life, the birth of her son and her becoming involved with the Church and a Bible study group. Of the latter she says, 'I had never read my Bible so this was a new experience for me. We began with Luke's Gospel and reached the verse where Jesus says to Peter: "From now on you will catch men." Then I dropped from overwork and exhaustion.' She continued:

My doctor said I had a depressive illness! He also said it would take a long time to get over it. However, I sat, while Peter had his daytime sleep and read my new Bible which my father had bought me for my 30th birthday and gave thanks for my illness, thanking the Lord that I could no longer do this and that and rush here and there. I so much needed rest and quiet to study the scriptures and learn more about God and what Jesus had done for me. Then one afternoon as I sat reading, I felt a presence in the room, one which I could almost reach out and touch, and somehow I knew this was the Holy Spirit and he spoke and said: 'Jesus did live, did die, rose again and lives today by the power of the Holy Spirit.' From that moment on I was changed. I had no idea what the experience was, I just knew that Jesus had come into my life and totally changed me and all I wanted to do was tell others about him and point them in his direction.

A lovely lay couple, Marie and Bernard, who are now with their Lord, looked after me in the early days of my pilgrimage and they identified the experience as the Baptism in the Holy Spirit. Yes, the very same that John the Baptist preached about. He said that Jesus was the one who would baptise in the Holy Spirit and with fire. Yes, there was a burning sensation within my chest and I was filled with an overwhelming sense of love for everybody and particularly my fellow Christians. It was rather like what colour television is after black and white.

Marie told me that after Bernard died she had to have a hip replacement. When she was baptised in the Holy Spirit some years earlier she had been completely healed of arthritis and she couldn't understand why she had to go into hospital for an operation when the Lord could heal her. But into hospital she went and she said she moaned and wailed in all her suffering and one day while in hospital, Jesus stood at the end of the bed and said, 'Look how I suffered,' and this humbled her so much she realised her sufferings were as nothing compared to his and her whole attitude changed and eventually she was able to live a normal life again, though sadly without Bernard at her side.

The remainder of the letter dealt with more general matters and her later life. It ended with: 'Hope I haven't bored you to death! God Bless and Much Love.'

## Assessment

These seven accounts of meetings with Jesus describe events that occurred between 1936 and 2001 which all took place in central England. It is likely that only one, or possibly two, of the writers would claim that they had been Christians at the moment of their revelations. The youngest, the 16-year-old Hugh Montefiore, was a member of a prominent Jewish family and had little interest in, or knowledge of, the Christian religion. But the experience was so powerful that it changed his life and he felt compelled to follow a path that grieved his family greatly – a decision he considered to be irrevocable. For the others, the changes that occurred following their meetings with Jesus may not have been so dramatic but were equally real – with one writing that 'Jesus had come into my life and totally changed me'.

My correspondents stressed the reality of the experiences in their letters. These events did not occur as dreams or in a hypnagogic state when they might have been unduly sleepy or drowsy, and none had taken hallucinatory drugs. They perceived the figure they truly believed was their risen Lord in a state of clear consciousness, and the impression was so powerful that it remained a vivid memory many years later. Yet they were not experiences that could be easily shared. The author of Letter 2 is quite explicit about this. She says, 'It has been very difficult to write these down, as this is the first time I've disclosed it. I hope they make sense.' Then she gives her reason for keeping them secret: 'On the face of it they might seem crazy, which is probably why I've kept quiet about them until now. Again I would ask anonymity if you use any of these stories.' People who have such unusual experiences are often frightened of going mad and/or of appearing foolish, but it is apparent from her letter that this woman is perfectly sane.

Bishop Montefiore gives a different reason for his reluctance to discuss what happened. He says in his autobiography: 'I find it hard to describe this experience, because words cannot do justice to it. Any verbal description sounds rather bare and banal. Deep religious experience is always indescribable, and usually incommunicable. I also fear that I may cheapen it by speaking of it too often. Not for one moment do I think this is a better way of becoming a Christian than any other. It was simply the way it happened to me, and it is still vivid in my memory, nearly sixty years later; and I have to begin this book by writing about it, because otherwise the rest of it would make no sense. It shaped the whole future of my life.' [3]

## What happened?

Some of the accounts are quite explicit; others more vague, but apart from Letter 3 where the Holy Spirit is specified, each respondent is certain that they have met Jesus in a special way. Moreover, the conviction that Jesus was present was instantaneous and sustained. This differs markedly from the failure of his followers to recognize him immediately when he appeared in the Garden and on the road to Emmaus. From a perspective of 2,000 years later, it is difficult to understand how people who had been with Jesus a few days before he died could fail to recognise him in his resurrected form, yet this is what we are told happened and Christians readily accept this. In contrast, when individuals claim to have met him in the 20th and 21st centuries, their claims are not likely to be taken seriously and their judgement or even truthfulness may be quietly questioned. This is not surprising, as they are telling of subjective impressions that cannot be confirmed and which other people find difficult to accept. However, this does not diminish the validity or importance of the encounter for the individual concerned. But sharing the experience can put a strain on personal relationships, as happened to Hugh Montefiore who found himself rejected by most family members (but not his father) when he became a Christian and chose to follow the path that the vision had shown for him.

Disagreements about the significance of numinous experiences is not a recent problem. Jesus' Resurrection and post-Ascension appearances proved to be possibly even more contentious 2,000 years ago, but many believed the disciples; hence the growth of Christianity.

Hugh Montefiore's vision was of a figure in white. He says it appeared in his 'mind's eye' and would not have appeared on a photograph if he had been able to take one. It was not a solid figure that could be touched, nor one that would walk alongside him as in the Gospel stories, nor did it appear with the intensity of the physical light that blinded Paul when he journeyed towards Damascus. Despite these differences, both men underwent a meaningful event that transformed their lives and they both heard a voice, though the language used was different in the two instances. The voice that questioned Paul probably spoke in Aramaic. The command to 'Follow me' that Hugh Montefiore received was given in English.

Paul's encounter with Jesus on the road to Damascus is mentioned three times in the Acts of the Apostles. One version says that Paul's companions heard the voice, but as a sound only (Acts 9: 3–9). That other people heard something suggests that the voice or sound was loud and was perceived by the normal process of hearing, not as an inner voice. In contrast, it seems likely that the words spoken to Hugh Montefiore were heard within and this may have been true for St Paul, despite the account given by Luke in Acts 9. I am told by my nephew Peter Cooke that where Paul wrote that 'God chose to reveal his Son in me' or 'within me' (Galatians 1: 15–16), the key word in the Greek text is *en emoi* and is dative and therefore static. Consequently it does not indicate a direction towards something or someone, as in 'towards me', and is more likely to refer to an inner voice. [4]

Similarly, the word 'Peace' as mentioned by the writer of Letter 2 was perceived not as an external sound but as something from within. It came, the writer says, 'straight into my being,' and is the only instance in which she said that Jesus spoke to her. It was not a quiet voice, not the 'still small voice' that Elijah heard when the Lord spoke to him (1 Kings 19: 12) but one of authority; 'yet most powerfully of all,' she says, 'was His Presence and His Voice.'

The woman who, we are told by the writer of Letter 3, saw Jesus standing at the foot of her hospital bed, was also addressed by a voice. She heard the words: 'Look how I suffered,' but we have no way of knowing if this was with her inner or outer ear, nor can we tell if Jesus appeared to her as the 'crucified' or the 'resurrected' Christ. The injunction 'Look how I suffered' suggests the former, though it could have been the risen Jesus emphasizing his identity with the Crucified One, as when he showed the disciples the marks of the nails in his hands and his feet.

Visions of the crucified Jesus are not unknown. They have been reported at various times and in many places: in the 20th century by Padre Pio in Italy [5] and by Dorothy Kerin in England. [6] A more recent and previously unrecorded account is given in Chapter 9 by a Muslim from Pakistan.

The emphasis given so far to the 'quiet inner voice' contrasts markedly with the experience of my first lay correspondent. 'Yet most powerfully of all,' she says, 'was His Presence and His Voice.' This indicates how unwise we are to try to limit his intentions and manifestations. She speaks also of the closeness of her relationship with him. She tells us that 'Several times His Presence and person has been very close to me, always with words to guide and always with a reassurance'. The relationship seems to be not fixed but developing and she speaks of becoming 'less aware of seeking Him, rather becoming part of His Presence'. She also speaks of a change in her prayer life whilst sitting in the cathedral. 'He was not there as Lord,' she says, 'yet I was in His Presence. I was experiencing prayer in another way, feeling that this is to lead me to be in His Presence at all times.'

## Differing perceptions

The impressions individuals retain of shared incidents, people or places rarely correspond exactly; their recollections and descriptions usually vary in some ways. Novelists have used this as a framework for stories, offering the reader different perspectives of a tragic or heroic event from the various angles provided by two or more observers. The differing ways in which the same incident can be interpreted, and remembered, is normal in the human condition and some would say that it helps to distinguish the human from the robotic mind. It is certainly evident in the Gospel accounts of the Resurrection. It is not surprising, therefore, that people's perceptions of the risen Jesus can vary greatly. Indeed, to complicate things, there are times when Jesus seems deliberately to manifest himself to people in a variety of ways, each suited to their own personality or spiritual needs. What is perhaps surprising are the many similarities present in the reports of such revelations that have come down to us over the centuries. We have already noted that Julian of Norwich said that visions of Jesus came to her in three ways: by physical sight, through words formed in the intellect, and spiritual sight. Theresa of Avila (1515–82), writing of her visions a hundred years after Julian, also described three types of perception. She said that sometimes the soul 'will feel Jesus Christ our Lord beside it. Yet it does not see Him, either with the eyes of the body or those of the soul'. This she called an 'intellectual vision'. [7] Then she states that: 'When our Lord is pleased to give more delight to the soul, He shows more clearly His most sacred humanity in the way He desires; either as He was when He went about the world or as He is after His Resurrection.' [8] This she called an 'imaginative vision', emphasizing that it is 'truly alive'. But the supreme experience she called the 'spiritual marriage'. Of this Theresa said: 'the delight of the soul is so extreme that I do not know what to compare it to…One can say no more than that the soul, I mean the spirit, is made one with God.' [9]

Even today people speak of being in the presence of Jesus. The writer of Letter 1 does so, as do various bishops in Chapters 4 and 5. For some, this is a subjective feeling only, but for others it is supported by physical perceptions – audible, tactile and/or visual – but whatever its form, it tends to have a directness and immediacy that leaves those affected in no doubt that they are in the presence of the ineffable.

Bishop Montefiore and my three lady correspondents all speak of having been in the presence of Jesus. For some it was a unique event, for others a more frequent happening. So how do they describe it? They do so usually with difficulty for, as the Bishop says, 'words cannot do justice to it' and they must seek to provide descriptions that they know are inadequate. If they choose to speak of it, and it is likely that many elect for silence instead (as the writer of Letter 2 indicates), they can only point to the experience, not depict it as it really happened with its full impact upon them.

When words are found, the struggle to explain may tend towards the repetitive. We find this tendency in Letter 1 where my correspondent writes, 'I believe with all my heart that the Presence I met was the Risen Lord,' and 'I became very aware of the Presence of the Risen Lord,' and 'Several times since, His Presence and person has been very close to me.' Similarly, in Letter 3 the correspondent writes, 'I felt a presence in the room, one that I could almost reach out and touch.' She does not say how she discerned the presence nor where she thought the voice ˙

came from, but she heard it say, 'Jesus did live, did die, rose again and lives today by the power of the Holy Spirit.' Somehow she knew that it was the Holy Spirit speaking. There was no doubt in her mind about this for she goes on to say, 'From that moment on I was changed. I had no idea what the experience was, I just knew that Jesus had come into my life and totally changed me.' This last statement is one that Evangelical Christians use quite often; it is implicit in the expression 'to be born again', but for those who have had no such experience the term can be incomprehensible, particularly as those who claim such experiences seldom find appropriate words to describe it adequately.

## The Visual Christ

It is apparent from the bishops' statements that a sense of the presence of Jesus is more common than a visual or auditory perception. When we compare the incidence of visual and auditory perceptions, the former appear to happen more frequently than the latter. This predilection will be explored further in a later chapter, but here we shall only consider the different ways in which Jesus manifested himself to my responders. We shall do this under the headings of light and physical appearance.

## His Appearance as Light

Christians are used to Jesus being perceived or described in terms of light. 'I am the Light of the World' is a description he applied to himself and it was as a 'blinding light' that he confronted Paul outside the city of Damascus, so there is no reason for us to be surprised if people say that in their meeting with Jesus they became aware of a brightness or a bright light. This claim is made by two of my lay correspondents and by one of the bishops. Both lay-women had met the risen Jesus more than once. Of her first meeting, the writer of Letter 1 says, 'His whole being was Light and white and he waited above the earth, not on the ground, yet in the room.' My second correspondent was more prosaic in her description. Of her second encounter, she says, 'There on the right side of the road was the Lord – very brightly I might say!' and of the third meeting: 'On my right, My Lord, tall and again, very bright.'

The figure of Jesus is not so clearly described in the reports provided by the bishops. The young Hugh Montefiore became aware of 'a figure in white' that appeared to him suddenly as he sat in a room by himself. It is possible that the figure may have been bathed or clothed in light, but one cannot be sure about the precise nature of the vision. We are on firmer ground with the statement made by another bishop who answered 'No' to question 3 but went on to say, 'But the time I said, "Lord, here am I, send me," on my knees in response to God's call, the room seemed blazing with light even though it was 1 a.m.' He also says, 'There have been many other special moments when I have been overwhelmed by Christ acting when things were impossible – and reassuring with words to my mind as a hug like a blanket.'

## His Physical Appearance

We have just seen Jesus described as one whose 'whole being was Light' and who waited 'above the earth, not on the ground'. This absence of direct contact with the earth contrasts with the picture of the Resurrected Jesus portrayed in the Gospels; it has more in common with people's concept of the ascended Christ and as such is unique amongst the cases that we have collected here. It is a form that artists often portray and it is also found in Phillip Wiebe's book *Visions of Christ* [10] where, in reporting Case 24 (Pauline Langlois), he wrote that 'Jesus appeared in the sky above her head. He appeared from the waist up and was surrounded by a very bright cloud. His form was so large it filled the sky'.

Here again, Jesus appears as more of an Ascension figure than as a man whose feet are firmly on the ground and who is ready to meet with, and talk to, other people. It was Ms Langlois' second visual experience and one that she categorized as a vision. (She refused to call her first experience a vision.) She said, 'It was very different. It was alive. It was like me and you...It was a man not a spirit.' A similar assessment is reported by Sundhar Singh in Chapter 9. He had many visions of Jesus but said that he had 'only seen Jesus once'.

Two correspondents speak of the physical stature of Jesus. The writer of Letter 1 says, 'His being is larger than ours, yet very real, not as a ghost or transient – yet most powerfully of all was His Presence and His Voice.' A different perspective is provided by the writer of Letter 2. This lady had three encounters with Jesus and mentions his physical appearance in two of her accounts. In the first she says, 'there was the Lord! A tall figure, not solid, stood in the room and simply held up His right arm as if to give a blessing.' Of the third meeting she writes, 'My Lord, tall and again, very bright. I remember such an overriding feeling of love – almost of being cuddled – coming from Him that I walked in His direction. He was with me for a moment as we walked together and then He was gone.' Both stress the reality of the experience whilst realizing that other people might have great difficulty in accepting that such a miraculous event could have happened in the 21st century.

It is interesting that the height of the perceived figure and the physical impact that it has can vary. If we accept the idea, if only as a point of discussion, that Jesus still appears to people as he did in the Gospel narratives, viz. in a discernibly human form, then we would expect his height to be within the normal range of human stature. That seems to be the case in most recorded instances. Of the 36 visions of Jesus reported by Wiebe [11], the figure of Christ is said to be of normal stature in 26 of them, with the remainder being larger-than-life figures. The description given in Letter 2, where Jesus is described as being 'tall', implies that the individual discerned is within the range of normal height and not unusually big.

Two letter writers give a hint of being almost touched. One speaks of 'almost being cuddled' whilst the other speaks of a presence that 'I could almost reach out and touch'. One bishop reports of Christ 'reassuring with words to my mind as a hug like a blanket'. These comments are suggestive but fall short of reporting actual physical contact. In contrast, haptic contact, in which the percipient does feel touched, is mentioned by nine of Wiebe's interviewees. Ernie Hollands was one such individual. A recidivist, he became well-known in Canada for his work with ex-offenders and in particular the establishment of Hebron Farm in 1983, as a Christian home for former prisoners. In 1975, Ernie was serving a long sentence for armed robbery when he awoke early one morning with the feeling that he should confess his sins to God. He was kneeling in prayer and weeping when he noticed that he was no longer in the cell but in a room with a door to his right through which Jesus had walked. Jesus stood in front of him and touched Ernie on his left shoulder (which he felt) and said three things to him. These were:

1) He was glad that Ernie did not kill the police officer he had shot.

2) That his slate was now wiped clean.

3) That he could now start all over again.

Jesus appeared to Ernie in traditional form: he was of medium height and dressed in white. When he spoke, his lips did not move but the words appeared to come from within Ernie himself [12]. This, as we have noticed, was the experience of Julian of Norwich and of the writer of Letter 2 who says that Jesus spoke to her 'not audibly but straight into my being'. I cannot be certain but I think it was also with this 'inner ear' that the two people mentioned in Letter 3 heard the words spoken to them.

## Ken is healed

Most encounters with Jesus involve just two people. Occasionally another person may be present as in Letter 2, where the car which was apparently miraculously dragged to safety, contained three people. A third person was also present when Ken Minter met Jesus, whom he speaks of as his 'mate'. The third person, Esmond (Jeff) Jefferies, had a significant role in the proceedings – he was also present when Donald English met Jesus, an encounter that will be discussed in the next chapter. I learnt about Ken from Jeff and was able to add to the information he provided by studying a videotape that Ken had recorded for the Pin Mill Christian Healing Fellowship. The videotape was recorded about 12 years after the main events took place. It is quite lengthy and not totally coherent [13].

Ken was probably in his forties when he sought help from Jeff Jefferies. Known locally as 'Ken the milk', he had been receiving treatment at the local hospital for an osteosarcoma of the right forearm. Seven courses of radiotherapy and two of chemotherapy had produced no obvious improvement and the pain in his arm was becoming unbearable. Then someone advised him to seek the help of a Christian healer, Jeff Jefferies, who lived near by. Not having any close connection to a church or chapel, this was a totally new idea to Ken but his response was immediate and straightforward. He said, 'I am ready to give it a go,' and arranged to see the healer. The healing session took place in Jeff's house. It started with a prayer and the laying on of hands, and as Ken was enjoying the warm, soothing feeling that came to him, he saw two ghost-like figures before him and a bright light to his right.

Describing the incident to Jeff on a videotape, he said, 'Then I

had this man with a big stick in his hand and this ball of fire...and
when you put your hands on my upper arm it got very hot again,
but what sticks in my mind is that when you brought your hands
down to the lower part of my arm the big bonfire I had seen was
just smouldering. The fire had gone and the smoke was in the
air...When I left the house I knew I would be healed.' He was
right. Later on the tape, he said, 'It was here, sitting in this chair,
that I met my mate Jesus who visited me in this room. He was
there to the right. I had a vision of this man with a great friendly
smile on his face. He was a very tall man with a white robe and
a staff in his hand. He just stood over me. Jesus was there, he
was there as large as life. He was there as clearly as I can see you
now. He was there to see that my cancer was blown away as I call
it. Jesus is there if you want help. I was cleaned, something was
washed away from me.'

## Changed lives

An analysis of the evidence suggests that a meeting with Jesus can
have both an immediate and a long-term effect. Hugh Montefiore
says of the immediate impact: 'It was an indescribably rich event
that filled me afterwards with overpowering joy.' The writers of
letters 1 and 3 rejoice in a sense of the presence, and the second
letter describes how the writer and her family were saved from
physical injury by the direct intervention of Jesus. Later she speaks
of a closer encounter where she feels his overpowering love and is
able to walk alongside him for a brief moment. Ken's experience
is more complex: he sees his mate Jesus but also a vivid mingling
of light and smoke and ash, and has the certainty of being healed
– an expectation that was justified by the outcome.

Two separate aspects are discernible in the long-term effects
of such encounters. These are a sense of continued support,
coupled with the certainty of change. Hugh Montefiore made

no conscious decision to become a Christian but he realized that it was a step that had to be taken. A similar outcome happened with Ken Minter and Ernie Hollands, and my three female correspondents speak of the way their lives were changed and of the continued support they receive. We learn from one that 'His Presence and person has been very close to me, always with words to guide and always with a reassurance', and from another that 'He was with me for a moment as we walked together and then He was gone. Maybe not really, as I'm sure that He carried me for the next few years'. In most cases these meetings produce a sense of uplift and support but this response is not invariable. The elderly lady, mentioned in Letter 3, who saw Jesus at the foot of her hospital bed, felt humbled by the vision. We are told that this brought about a change in her attitude to her arthritic illness and that she was eventually able to live a normal life again. It is unlikely that her physical disabilities were cured – chronically distorted arthritic joints do not regain their normal function and appearance – but at least she regained her inner harmony and probably learnt to cope with the situation more effectively.

## In the slums

This chapter contains nine separate accounts, given by six people, of their meetings with Jesus. We started with a bishop and conclude with the words of Charles Raven, former Regius Professor of Divinity at Cambridge. The incident occurred when the young Raven was visiting a friend at Stoke-on-Trent. The friend was a curate and Raven said, 'I was used to slums, but for brute ugliness Stoke and its vast and dismal churchyard stand unique. My friend was ill; I wandered up to his rooms alone, and the grim tragedy of the place struck me cold with misery. He had loved the country, and music, and all beautiful things, and he was living in this hell. I found him, and behold he was not alone. No other phrase will express it. Here walking with him in the midst of the furnace was Jesus, and its flames were an aureole. He had found that which together we had sought. Jesus was alive and present to my friend as he had been to the eleven in the upper room. He was alive and present to me. I had studied the evidence for Resurrection with an unbeliever's critical scrutiny and had been persuaded of its validity but not of its consequences. Now I knew. It was not a dream for Saul of Tarsus, nor for a multitude of disciples through the ages. It was no longer a dream for me: for here was the reality of it. Such is a summary of the crucial event of my life.' [14]

With this depiction of Jesus accompanying his friend 'in the midst of the furnace', Raven draws our attention, unintentionally but implicitly, to the biblical story of the three youths who were cast into a burning fiery furnace and were joined by a 'fourth man' who protected them from the flames and secured their release (Daniel 3: 22 ff). The newcomer is often perceived, especially in Eastern Orthodox texts, as portraying the presence of Jesus in the fire, and as providing a prophetic indication of his and our own Resurrection from death and Hell. [15] This relationship between someone's experience of meeting Jesus and biblical events is not unusual; the pattern is often evident and some of the meetings recorded here – for instance, Jesus entering the room and speaking the word 'Peace'; Jesus standing at the bedside of an elderly woman; Jesus appearing as light and speaking words that altered the direction of a young man's life – are readily identifiable with accounts recorded in the New Testament.

# CHAPTER 7

# Deathbed Experiences

EATH AND CHILDBIRTH HAVE much in common. They are defining moments in a person's life and both represent a new beginning for the individual concerned. Doctors and nurses are usually present at these critical times; clergy less frequently, but when they are present it is because the family understands the spiritual significance of the occasion. Three bishops sent me comments that are relevant to the deathbed scene, the most apposite being the shortest. The bishop wrote: 'There is often a deep consciousness of the risen Christ coming to take his Child home – at the time of death – very moving to be there.'

Bishop Morris Maddocks expressed it differently. In a letter (mentioned already in Chapter 5 as Bishop 34), he wrote of a parishioner who was so critically ill in hospital that the surgeon phoned to advise the bishop to visit the man that night, rather than in the morning. Bishop Morris reacted quickly. He collected his oils and hurried with his wife to the hospital where he found the patient in an oxygen tent, scarcely able to speak. In the presence of his wife and a nurse, the bishop had the curtains around the bed closed and anointed the man. In his book, *The Christian Healing Ministry*, he says of the same incident that, 'When the nurse drew the curtains back after the service, the men on the opposite side of the ward beckoned me over. They silenced my attempts at an apology and said that they did not know what had happened behind the curtain, but something had and they knew he'd be all right.' Later, the sister told the bishop that a remarkable change came over the men in the ward following the anointing. There was a new atmosphere of caring and concern for others, and most of the bad language ceased. [1] The man did well and was back at work in a fortnight. He died two years later, but the bishop wrote: 'He glowed for those two years and the men in the ward were right. The risen Christ was present and raised him up.'

Charles Raven experienced the reality of the risen Christ in a different way, when he visited a sick friend in Stoke-on-Trent in the 1920s. His account is given towards the end of the previous chapter and, though he does not say that the friend was dying, it seems likely that the man was close to death. The impact the visit had on Professor Raven was so great that he called it 'the crucial event of my life' and said he was certain that he had been in the presence of Jesus and that Jesus was alive. He was equally sure that Jesus had been as present to his friend 'as he had been to the eleven in the upper room'.

These two encounters with Jesus are both interesting and unusual. Deathbeds are rarely the scene of dramatic events and visions of Christ are not expected or sought within the sickroom. On such occasions, people look for a quiet and peaceful end to life and this becomes an increasingly relevant hope as we grow older. In his autobiography *Oh God, What Next?* [2], Bishop Hugh Montefiore writes of the peacefulness surrounding the death of his 81-year-old mother. He speaks of her prolonged illness and how her demise was the first occasion when he held someone's hand as they died. Then he adds: 'Her death was the most peaceful thing in the world: she simply stopped breathing.' One senses a note of surprise in those words, as though the bishop did not expect death to be so easy. But the last hours of life are usually tranquil and a peaceful death is the most natural and common end of life. It differs markedly from the pain and distress that can dominate the early phases of a terminal illness if adequate care is not provided.

These peaceful transitions, though common, are not well documented. Some are described in *Deathbed Visions* by Sir William Barrett, whilst Edward Robinson's *Living The Questions* contains a memorable account of the last hours of a clergyman's life, though the account does not include a specifically Christian vision. [3] At a different level, I remember talking to a Catholic nun, a member of the Medical Missionaries of Mary, who had seen many people die in the refugee camps of Central Africa. She said that the deaths were invariably peaceful, even among the emaciated.

## Islam

The birth of a child is always a joyful occasion. When a baby signals its entry into the physical world with its first cry, every face lightens and there is an almost palpable sense of relief and happiness. Death produces a different reaction. Even if the person's death is long expected – perhaps even desired for that person's sake – there is always a lowering of mood in the room or hospital ward. These are universal experiences that cross every cultural and religious boundary.

I have been involved with the care of only a few Muslim patients but I remember one most vividly. The man had cancer of the kidney and I recall walking upstairs with a MacMillan nurse to the bedroom where he lay. The room was full of men; only one woman was present and she was the man's wife. There must have been over twenty people in the bedroom and everyone was quiet and still. The man's son stood by the bedside; we talked quietly together, then he would translate and explain our conversation to an older man, presumably the senior family member present in the room. The family had decided to keep the patient at home and, although he had only a few hours to live, they wanted to ensure that he received all the appropriate care that was available.

He died a few hours after we had left and his body was flown to Pakistan for burial. Visiting that patient gave me a brief insight into the way people of other cultures behave in the presence of death. The atmosphere was peaceful, respectful and spiritual in the sense that they knew that they were witnessing not just the end of a life but a stage of transition for a human soul.

Islam teaches that the angels Munkar and Nakir receive the soul at death and assign it a place in the afterlife. There it remains until the Final Day of Judgement when the souls are reunited with their bodies, the dead come out of their graves and everyone is judged by Allah. It is because of their sure belief in the physical Resurrection of the dead that Muslims, in common with Orthodox Jews and some Christian sects, bury their dead and forbid the cremation of the corpse. A people's attitude to cremation is a good indication of the way they perceive the afterlife. Cremation is not only allowed, but is the traditional method of disposal for Hindus, Jains and Sikhs – people who believe in reincarnation and who do not consider the physical Resurrection of the individual to be true or relevant. Cremation is also widely used by those who are convinced that there is no life beyond death.

In Christian countries, a major change in attitude to cremation began at the end of the 19th century and became established early in the 20th century. Before then, burial was the normal and only permissible way of disposing of the dead. Today, burial is relatively uncommon in many of those countries and cremation is normal practice. Existing legal sanctions against cremation have been repealed and these changes have been accepted by Christian denominations with varying degrees of enthusiasm. This change in burial practise reflects a changed attitude to the afterlife in the West. In Western Christianity the credal belief in the 'Resurrection of the body' used to imply a belief in the ultimate reanimation of the physical body. This is no longer the case, and increasingly Christians tend to believe that eternity is not earth bound and that the dead will be resurrected in a spiritual body, not one that can be carbon-dated. It must be said that the Church's teaching on this subject is not clear and, as the different views expressed by the bishops in Chapter 5 indicate, needs to be clarified.

We know very little about the deathbed visions that may occur in Muslim communities, as no research appears to have been done into this aspect of Muslim life. However, the incidence is likely to be the same as in other societies though the cultural content will probably differ. We will see later in this chapter that some Christians have visions of Jesus when they die – St Stephen was the first person to do so – but whilst Muslims hold Jesus in high esteem, it is unlikely that any deathbed visions Muslims might have would feature Jesus.

We know from the work of Osis and Haraldsson that the incidence of deathbed visions people have is the same among Christians and Hindus but that the content differs. Hindus usually see deities from their own pantheon of gods [4] and similar experiences can be expected among Jews and Muslims, but it is unwise to speculate about the forms they may take as we lack adequate data. We do not know, for instance, if the prohibition against artistic portrayals in Islam means that visions of the Prophet Muhammad never occur or, alternatively, if they do occur, whether the individuals are aware that the visions are of Muhammad. If they do occur, another possibility is that the experiences are consciously repressed and never openly admitted, because to deify any person, including Muhammad, is the most heinous sin in Islam.

## Resuscitation

Throughout the ages, all races and religions have responded to the needs of the dying with particular care, demanding respect for the body and enhanced support for the bereaved. Traditional forms of care have been formulated but these are not fixed, and the mourning and burial procedures that we see practised in Western countries differ greatly from those that were the norm 100 years ago. These changes are not confined to First World countries; they are to be seen throughout the world.

One recent development has been the widespread use of cardiopulmonary (CP) resuscitation when the death has been sudden and unexpected. CP resuscitation, i.e. a combination of mouth-to-mouth breathing and external cardiac massage, can be administered in almost any situation and First Aid services are well versed in the practice. The method has its possible origins in a technique mentioned in the Old Testament, where we are told that the prophets Elijah and Elisha each restored a dead person to life. The first incident involved Elijah, who resuscitated a young boy by mouth-to-mouth respiration (1 Kings 17: 21-22).

The account given of Elisha's healing is more detailed, and combined breathing into the mouth with rhythmic compression of the chest. A lad had gone into the fields to watch the reapers work and whilst there, complained of a severe pain in the head. He was taken home and died in his mother's arms. She went immediately to Elisha who hurried back to the house with her – only to find the boy lying dead on his bed. The prophet shut the door and prayed. Then: 'He lay upon the child, put his mouth to the child's mouth, his eyes to his eyes, and his hands on his hands; and, as he pressed upon him, the child's body grew warm. Elisha got up and walked once up and down the room; then getting on the bed again, he pressed upon him and breathed into him seven times; and the boy opened his eyes. (2 Kings 4: 34-35, *New English Bible*.)

The techniques used by the prophets have had their critics and supporters. I remember, for instance, being told by a senior obstetrician in London in 1955, never to use positive pressure techniques to resuscitate the newborn, and being informed by Dr Tony Paddon in Labrador, in 1959, that he had never lost a newborn infant because he had always used mouth-to-mouth resuscitation at their births. CP resuscitation was shown to be effective and became widely accepted for modern use only as recently as the early 1960s. Since then many lives have been saved that previously would have been lost.

One consequence of CP interventions is that individuals sometimes report having had an out-of-the-body experience while in the transition stage between life and death. This phenomenon, which can occur for other reasons and is well-documented, is now referred to as a near-death experience. [5, 6] The content of the experiences varies, but some people report seeing an individual that they can identify as Jesus. George Ritchie was one such person. [7] Ritchie had a cardiac arrest in 1943 whilst serving as a GI in the US Army. He was resuscitated and had a near-death experience during which he found himself in the presence of Jesus. Because of his meeting with Jesus, Ritchie was convinced that he had been restored to life 'to become a physician so that I could learn about man and then serve God'. After his release from the army he went to medical school, trained as a physician and became a leading psychiatrist in the US. Raymond Moody, author of *Life after Life*, was one of his students, and it was largely due to the encouragement that he received from Ritchie that Moody undertook the pioneering work on near-death experiences that made him a household name when he published his results in 1975.

Near-death experiences can vary greatly in content, but usually they involve a feeling of peace and painlessness and sometimes an out-of-the-body experience occurs. Other experiences are reported also. These include a life review: travelling rapidly through a tunnel and meeting other beings who may include

Jesus. In this last instance, people may say that they have been sent back to continue their lives in this world. The return is often painful and not desired. The first time I encountered this phenomenon was in an account given by an Anglican priest who had been severely injured in a road traffic accident in South Africa and was admitted to hospital clinically dead. He experienced an initial sense of painlessness, then of travelling rapidly through space where he was met and sent back to his body as he was resuscitated – feeling great pain after he re-entered the body. He attributed his recovery to his congregation having learnt of the accident and then praying fervently for his safe return.

Another incident which comes to mind was related by a nursing sister at a seminar I was leading. The sister told of an instance when she had returned to her duties following a few days' regular leave. As soon as she entered the ward, a woman called her to her bedside and thanked her fervently for the care she had received from the ward sister when she was being resuscitated. The woman had been admitted to the ward as an emergency. Soon after admission her heart stopped beating and a resuscitation team was called in to help. She was given CP resuscitation and during the whole process she was outside her body and aware of the actions being taken by the nursing and medical staff. During the resuscitation, the ward sister had been very careful to ensure that the woman's most intimate parts were kept covered. Since her personal dignity had been maintained, even though she had been unconscious, the woman felt especially grateful to the ward sister.

## Buddhist practices

One consequence of the changing attitudes to death of modern societies is the diminishing spiritual support provided in the last moments of life. This is true not only in the West; it is also evident in China and other Asian countries. For Orthodox Christians, the Eastern Church does provide a beautiful 'Office of the Parting of the Soul from the Body' which is said as death approaches, and the Last Rites are available in the Catholic Church. However, Christian ministers in the Reformed Churches are less likely to be present at a deathbed scene (Rabbis of the Jewish Orthodox synagogues very rarely attend), and some seem uncertain about the best way to handle the situation. Nor do they have a coherent view to offer on what happens to the individual after death. In this area the clergy seem no more assured than the laity and are perhaps less free to consider the spiritual and psychological issues involved. They appear to be more tentative and psychologically less well equipped than Buddhist leaders, whose training and meditative practices provide them with different insights into the nature of life and death.

Buddhists start with the premise that every moment involves the death and rebirth of consciousness and that this is a constant cycle throughout life. However, the moment of physical death is of particular importance to Buddhists, not just because of the grief it brings to loved ones, but because they consider that a person's state of mind at that precise instant helps to determine the quality of their subsequent state of being. Buddhists consider that the presence of monks (clergy) at the moment of death, or as soon as possible afterwards, is an essential aid to a good death. (This was a practice that was common among Christians but is no longer observed in the Christian faith with any frequency.) As death approaches, the Buddhist is helped to be in as virtuous a state of mind as possible, for this is the moment when the most profound and beneficial experiences can occur, and the dying have been taught to see it as a means of gaining spiritual realization. For this reason, Buddhists who meditate regularly try to continue doing so for as long as possible while they pass through the moment of death into the post-death state that they call *bvanga*. This they regard as a neutral state, like sleep, in which there is conscious activity but no awareness. According to different authorities the *bvanga* may last for any period from a few hours to 40 days.

I was most impressed by an incident involving the Buddhist teacher Sogyal Rinpoche when he visited St Mary's Hospice in Birmingham in the early 1980s. It was before he wrote his spiritual classic *The Tibetan Book of Living and Dying* and when he was still relatively unknown. His aides had arranged the visit and the hospice staff were looking forward to hearing him speak, but when he eventually arrived he spoke very briefly and offered to answer questions. Then I showed him around the hospice, but when we reached the men's ward I stopped at the entrance and did not take him inside. This was because a new patient had just been admitted to a bed by the door and was obviously close to death. After we had completed a tour of the hospice, Rinpoche insisted on returning to the ward where the dying man lay and stood about six feet from the foot of the bed, looking at him very intently for some time. His appearance seemed to change and he ceased to be the young man that I had conducted around the hospice; his face and body language becoming that of a much older, wiser individual. He said nothing and I have no idea what was going through his mind, but I am quite sure that he was supporting in some way the passing of that man and that what he was doing was important. I may add that I have been present quite frequently when Christian clergy have ministered at deathbeds, but I have never seen anyone whose effect was as moving as was Rinpoche's on that silent occasion. It is likely that he was using a practice called *phowa* which Buddhists employ when in the presence of the dying. I had not encountered it previously but I know that it is not 'faith limited' and can be used to help people of any, or no, religious belief during a terminal illness. It is essentially a form of silent prayer, or invocation, and is described in Sogyal Rinpoche's book. [8]

Rinpoche says that if Christians wish to use *phowa* to help the dying, they should sit quietly at the bedside and follow their own spiritual practice in terms of prayer, Bible reading and the use of candles or icons. They should visualize the risen Jesus above the head of the patient radiating light onto them, purifying his or her whole being and enabling them to merge into the spiritual presence. He advises: 'Do this practice throughout your loved one's illness, and especially (and most important), as soon as possible after breathing stops and before the body is touched or disturbed in any way. If the dying person knows that you are going to do this practice for them, and knows what it is, it can be a great source of inspiration and comfort.'

## The last moments

Buddhists consider it important to help others to die well. So do Christians and people of other faiths, and though we may differ in our ideas on how best to achieve it, our objectives are the same. Usually there are three main areas of concern: the patient's physical distress, their mental and emotional distress, and their spiritual needs. The first requirement is to make sure that the individual is free from physical discomfort or needs. Good nursing and medical care are basic requirements, and this is the time when the expertise of specialists in palliative care can be most helpful. The second concern, to ease any mental or emotional distress, is an area in which family and friends are invaluable. They will have had many years' experience of the patient but, paradoxically, their involvement is not always welcomed, partly because of their own grief and need for support, and partly because the care of the dying has been relocated from the home to the hospital or hospice and is no longer considered primarily a family concern but a job for healthcare workers.

Despite the involvement and expertise of hospital chaplains, providing spiritual support for the dying patient and their family is perhaps the most neglected area of care in hospitals. Yet it is so important. I have seen it provided most beautifully by a MacMillan nurse, when in her role as a Minister of the Sacrament she visited a dying patient at home to take her the Blessed Sacrament. Five of us were present and little was said, yet I cannot find the words to describe the atmosphere of that simple service. In contrast, when my dearest wife died after a few days' illness in hospital, the spiritual support provided within the unit was nil. Her last few days were spent in an intensive care unit where she was so enwrapped by intravenous drips, a ventilator and other accessories that it was impossible to get close to her. The nurses and junior doctors caring for her did their best to prolong her life, and I am grateful for their efforts, but it was very clinical and they seemed to have very little support at a senior level as they managed Valerie's fluid balance and biochemical needs. It was an open ward with other patients present, and I have never felt more distanced from a person in my professional or private life. I felt unable to approach my wife, to speak to her or to touch her. That particular unit was scheduled to be closed down permanently so it was not typical of its genre, and although as a family we were greatly upset, we realized that the staff were doing their best.

Few people die as atheists or as convinced agnostics. In my experience, only two people have died without some expectation that there is, or might be, a life beyond death. Sigmund Freud, the founder of psychoanalysis, claimed to be an atheist but he also formulated the theory of 'unconscious immortality', which states that 'in the unconscious everyone is convinced of his/her own immortality'. [9] It means that 'people are genetically programmed to be believers' and that as death approaches they expect that something meaningful will follow afterwards. For many, this may be a reunion with their loved ones and/or a closer meeting with God; others are simply content to rest in the hands of a divine providence that they rarely bothered about during life but always trusted to conduct them through its difficulties.

I am reminded of an old lady, bed-ridden with arthritis, who spoke of occasions when she felt the hands of Jesus raise her out of the body and relieve all her pains. I cannot explain the mechanics of these events but they may have been early stages of a near-death experience when some aspect of the individual – her spirit or soul – loosened its links with the body and became able to explore regions that are not normally accessible to the conscious mind.

## Deathbed visions of Jesus

Most of us have special experiences that act as beacons on our spiritual journey. They appear at different times and places but the ones that occur at a deathbed are of particular significance. These impressed the bishop whose remark about 'Christ's presence at the time of death' is quoted at the beginning of this chapter. I can identify with his comment, but the likelihood of being aware of such a presence varies with location. I know that my own awareness of the spiritual significance of a death is much greater in the person's home than elsewhere. In my experience it is less marked in a hospice, scarcely noticeable in hospitals and never apparent at the site of a suicide or accidental death.

Some incidents stand out clearly in my recollection and one involved a patient of a partner. A quiet, pleasant woman, she was a regular church-goer who rarely consulted a doctor. One night I received an urgent call to visit and, as was the custom in those days, went immediately to see her. It was a terraced house with the living room immediately to the right of the entrance. She was lying on a small couch in the living room and a single glance was sufficient to show that she was dead. Her husband was an officer in the St John's Ambulance Brigade and was used to dealing with medical emergencies, but her death came as a total shock to him. It seems that everything had appeared to be normal when they had gone to bed, but soon after retiring she got up and went downstairs. She gave no explanation for doing this, but almost immediately afterwards she called out to him: 'Come down quickly, I am dying. I can see Jesus.' He hurried down the stairs but by the time he reached her there was nothing he could do to help; she could not be roused. I found the whole situation very moving and realised there was little that I could do. I had a statutory duty to inform the coroner, which could wait until morning, but in the meantime there was the need to lay out the body. The incident occurred in a small country town where the district nurse was also the midwife and was not allowed to handle dead bodies. The funeral director worked on a part-time basis and could provide no service at night so I laid out the body myself. This was the only occasion that I did anything of that sort and it proved to be a surprisingly moving thing to undertake, probably because of the circumstances associated with her death.

I wonder how often people see Jesus at the moment of their death? Such incidents do occur but not frequently. Few reports were available until Moody's book appeared in the 1970s, but among the earliest was a book on deathbed visions by Sir William Barrett, a former President of the Royal Society and a physicist. His book records fifty deathbed visions but only one involved Jesus. This happened to Daisy Dryden, a 10-year-old girl who died in San Jose, California in 1864. Daisy was recovering from a fever when her father, who was sitting on her bed, noticed a sudden change of expression in her face. Her eyes became fixed on a spot above the door and her face assumed an expression of amazement and pleasure. He asked, 'What is it?' and she replied, 'It is a spirit, it is Jesus, and He says I am going to be one of His little lambs.' She added, 'Oh Papa, I am going to Heaven, to Him.' That night she had a relapse and died a few days later.

Daisy remained mentally alert until the end and when she heard someone speak of the dark river that she would soon cross, her response was immediate and emphatic. 'There is,' she said, 'no river; there is no curtain; there is not even a line that separates this life from the other life.' Then gesturing with her hands, she said, 'It is here and it is there; I know it is so, for I can see you all, and I see them there at the same time.' When asked to describe what she saw, she replied, 'I cannot describe it; it is so different, I could not make you understand.' [10]

Daisy's response reminds me of a remark an elderly lady made to me as I was leaving her house. It had been more of a social than a medical visit and we had chatted mainly about her dead husband, but as I left she said, 'Doctor, the veil is much thinner than people realize.' She died a few days later quite unexpectedly, which gave her parting words a greater significance for me.

The Christian healer and stigmatist Dorothy Kerin also wrote of Jesus being present at her mother's death. Mrs Kerin died at Chapel House, then the centre of Dorothy's healing ministry before she moved to Burrswood in Kent. Of her mother's death, Dorothy wrote: 'She was given one of the most lovely passings that I have ever witnessed. It was literally a falling asleep in Jesus. A short time before this she had a vision, during which her face was so indescribably lovely and shining with light that several people came into the room to pray. It was felt by all that the Beloved Lord was there. She regained consciousness after this, and I asked her if she knew me. She replied: "Yes, I am healed, I have seen Jesus. He told me things about you. He said, 'I will never leave her.'" Those were her last words.' [11]

## Cultural components of visions

In 1977 Osis and Haraldsson published a cross–cultural survey of deathbed visions. [4] The study, which was conducted simultaneously in the United States and India, had two aims: first to assess the accuracy of a pilot survey that had been undertaken in 1959–60; and second to gather more detailed data. The survey recorded case histories and visions from 877 individuals – 442 resident in the US and 435 in India. Doctors and nurses who had cared for these people were asked to complete a questionnaire and then be interviewed on the basis of their replies. In the US the interviews were conducted by telephone; in India mostly by direct personal contact. Of the 877 patients who were enrolled in the survey, 471 proved to be terminally ill and thus suitable for inclusion in the final analysis of data.

The study was important for its pioneering work. It may have methodological flaws (*viz.* respondents were interviewed differently in the US and India) but it does provide an insight into the types of experience that can occur during the last few hours of life. It shows that people who are close to death may be aware of the presence of deities, saints and relatives who have died. The perceptions are mainly visual, are of short duration and occur mostly (65%) during the last few minutes of life. Osis and Haraldsson consider the visions to be 'survival related' because most patients believe that the visitor has come to 'take them away' to another realm of life, and because their response is usually one of serenity, peace or elation (71%). The survey showed that the likelihood of a person having a deathbed vision was not affected by variables such as age, sex, educational level, occupation, race or religious belief, though the latter is likely to give a cultural orientation to the contents of the vision. Indian patients, for instance, usually report seeing Hindu religious deities. Americans are more likely to see dead relatives and to report the presence of Jesus, the Blessed Virgin Mary and other Christian saints.

Visions and dreams may be culturally influenced in other ways. For instance a Hindu doctor who I visited during his terminal illness, spoke of dreaming about a garden which was full of the most wonderful fruit trees. There were no flowers in the garden and, for some reason that I could not understand, the abundance of fruit trees and the absence of flowers was important to him. It was a happy and significant dream for the dying man. A different type of vision was related by the wife of a doctor shortly before she died of breast cancer. They were practising Catholics and she was very angry at the prospect of dying in her early 50s when she felt she had much more life to live and experience. But her attitude changed during the last 24 hours of life when she had a dream in which she saw herself as the bride of Christ being prepared for her marriage. This is the only time that I have encountered a *hierosgamos* – a dream in which there is a sacred marriage or death wedding. Psychologists say that although uncommon it is highly significant. The Jungian psychologist Marie-Louise von Franz [12] says it is an archetypal motif indicating 'a union of opposites'; a typical example being the portrayal of Christ and the Church as bridegroom and bride. In this particular case, the dream pointed to the woman's ultimate union with Christ.

## Dr English sees Jesus

Deathbed visions are seen in the last moments, or hours, of life by the dying person. Much less frequently they may be seen by people attending the sick person. The Rev Dr Donald English was one such person. His clear description of the incident and his prominent role within the Methodist Church gives this account of Jesus appearing in a sick room added significance. Donald English was notable in many ways, both within and outside the Church. He was a well-known lecturer and broadcaster, twice President of the Methodist Conference of Great Britain, Chairperson of the World Methodist Council (1991-6) and Moderator of the Free Church Federal Council (1986-7). He died in August 1998, 13 months after the death of his wife, Bertha.

Bertha had metastatic cancer of the liver. After the diagnosis was made, she lived for a few months at home where she received healing from Esmond Jefferies, a Christian healer and friend of the couple. During two of these healing sessions, Dr English realized that Jesus was present in the room, though he kept this knowledge secret for some months, not even mentioning it to his friend. He probably spoke of it for the first time in a lecture to Methodist students at Cliff College in central England. This occasion was described by Christine Scott, a Methodist preacher and finalist in *The Times* Best Sermon competition of 1998. In her sermon, which was published in *The Times Book of Best Sermons*, she told of attending a lecture where Dr English spoke of his wife's illness and how he and a friend had prayed for her. She remembered him saying: 'There were three people in the room, but as they prayed he saw four and Jesus was there with them. Their friend came on another occasion and again there were three people present, but again Dr English saw four. Jesus was there with them once more. It was as if Jesus had come to see what they were doing, to say: That's fine. That's OK. But I'll be back.' [13]

Esmond Jefferies learnt of Donald's experiences by a different route. He had asked his friend to write an article for a Christian Healing Fellowship journal called *Lifeline*. Donald did so and wrote of his wife's illness as follows: 'There were times during her illness, and there have been for me since, when the signals of divine presence were deeply surprising as well as comforting and challenging. At times such signals were almost overpowering, not least two occasions involving a vision of the risen Christ in the room.' He added, 'I don't find that easy to write, since I am not a person whose Christian life has been marked by such experiences.' [14]

The article gave Esmond his first indication that Donald had seen Jesus when he himself was ministering to his friend's wife. He spoke to Donald on the 'phone to ask what he meant by 'the risen Christ in the room', and to enquire why he had not been told before, even though he was present on those memorable occasions. In answer to the latter question, he was told: 'I didn't know what to expect, but even if I had tried to speak about it I could not have done so. I would have been too emotional.'

The men arranged to meet again some weeks later at Donald's home in the Cotswolds, in the house where Jesus had appeared. Esmond used the opportunity to obtain more details from his friend. He wanted to know exactly what Donald had seen and if it was a ghostly or transparent figure. They went upstairs to the bedroom and relived the moments when they sat facing each other across Bertha's bed with Donald facing the door and Jefferies giving her healing. Donald described what had happened in this way: 'After you had given the prayer of healing for Bertha, I looked up, and there, standing by the dressing table, was the figure,' pointing as he spoke to the exact spot where the figure had stood. He said it was not a ghostly or transparent figure but 'a solid figure, as solid as I can see you now. It was not quite so clearly defined as I see you, but there was no doubt who it was.' He knew that it was Jesus Christ. The figure did not speak aloud but it seemed to Donald that he was saying, 'You are doing the right thing. Carry on and when the time is right, I will be back.' Donald said that 'Jesus stood there for about 3-4 minutes and then walked out through the door. He did not suddenly vanish or gently fade away, he just walked out of the door.' [15]

In their later discussions, Donald English said that if it had happened to anyone else, he would have doubted whether it really had occurred. He likened his scepticism to the way Bible Study classes might discuss the Transfiguration and come to the conclusion that the disciples' perception of Moses and Elijah alongside Jesus was some sort of 'inner vision'. But having had his own experience, he no longer had any hesitation in accepting the disciples' account of what had happened.

Dr English's revelation is unusual, yet two similar incidents are associated with the Pin Mill Christian Healing Fellowship in East Anglia. The first occurred when Esmond Jefferies laid hands on Ken Minter as reported in the preceding chapter. The other incident involved not Esmond, but two other members of the Fellowship. In both cases only the person receiving healing saw the figure of Christ. Of this, Esmond made the following comment: 'In such cases there is always an element of doubt that creeps in. Did those people imagine the presence of Christ? But when Donald says that he saw the figure standing there for three to four minutes, I am left in absolutely no doubt that Jesus was there just as he promised he would be "Where two or three come together in my name".' [15]

So did this perception of Jesus make any difference to Donald and Bertha in the last months of their lives? No clear answer is given to the question and we do not know if Bertha was informed of the visitations, but we are told that she 'had always been sensitive to the ways in which God's presence is perceivable, if you're looking', and of himself, Donald says he was 'almost overpowered' by such 'signals of the divine presence'. Of the illness, he is certain that 'prayer and laying on of hands made a difference' and wrote that Bertha spoke openly about her impending death, 'believing that Jesus would keep his promise and come and take her to himself.' [16]

Dr English's standing in the Church gives added interest to the report. So does the detailed precision of his comments and his initial reluctance to speak of his experiences. His former ambiguous attitude to the Transfiguration suggests that his more recent experiences were not likely to have been wish-fulfilling fantasies. The appearance of the Christ figure on two separate occasions adds interest to his account. That Donald English was not the patient but a caring relative is also significant: it makes any suggestion that he might have been hallucinating as a consequence of an illness or its treatment less tenable. Most importantly, he saw the figure as a real man of normal build and appearance, yet totally recognizable as Jesus. He did not see a supernatural figure or body of light, but someone who was clearly human.

## Possible explanations

Deathbed visions take various forms. They are sometimes classified as near-death experiences, though the distinction is obvious and should be maintained. We do not know how often they occur and they are not mentioned in Professor Wiebe's important book *Visions of Jesus,* but it is an aspect of human experience that has interested me for many years. There are three reasons for this long-standing interest, one of which has been mentioned already – the urgent call to her husband of: 'Come down quickly. I am dying, I can see Jesus,' from the woman who realized she was dying. Obviously a rational explanation needs to be sought for such a happening, but whilst various suggestions have been offered, none provides a satisfactory answer.

Among the explanations given for phenomena of this sort, the following are typical. It has been suggested that the woman's vision of Jesus was caused by her illness, the drugs she was prescribed, hypoxia, or by a sudden release of endorphins – the endogenous opioids produced by the body as a response to pain. None of these explanations are sustainable in this instance. The woman had no medically recorded illness, and on the night she died she had gone to bed perfectly well. She was taking no medically prescribed drugs and was not an alcoholic. She was not in pain and had no difficulty breathing. At the inquest, the coroner reached a verdict of death from natural causes. Regarding the vision, there is no reason to doubt the woman's own assessment that Jesus had appeared to her. If an acceptable biomedical explanation becomes available it might clarify uncertainties, but it would not of necessity exclude the possibility of a spiritual factor being involved.

## My mother's death

The second reason for my interest in deathbed visions is more personal. I was with my mother when she died of ovarian cancer in August 1964. Just the two of us were present, my father having died of cardiac failure five weeks earlier. Both deaths occurred in my home in mid-Wales. My mother's illness was protracted, with a lot of pain over a period of 18 months. This was before the practice of palliative medicine was established, and few doctors provided terminal cancer patients with adequate pain relief. I had great respect for the attending physician, and during the thirteen years we worked together I learnt much from him, but in retrospect the amount of opiates he gave my mother was negligible and she had no analgesics at all during the last 24 hours of her life. So what happened could not have been due to drugs.

During the last brief phase of her life, I was sitting at my mother's bedside. We were alone and she was unconscious, when suddenly she sat up and opened her arms wide as if to embrace someone. That was surprising in itself, but more remarkable was the changed appearance of her face. It lost the pallor and sunken expression of the dying and simply radiated with light and joy. This lasted for a short time only, then she lay back, turned towards me and said, 'Bye, bye, *cariad*,' (a Welsh term of endearment). I was too distressed to stay in the room and left to regain my composure. When I returned shortly afterwards, she was dead.

What had happened in those brief moments was quite unique in my life as a doctor and I did not meet anyone who had had a similar experience until 1989 when I spoke at a conference at St Joseph's Hospice, London. About a hundred people were present at the meeting. There were a few doctors but most were nurses and other health care workers interested in palliative care. The audience was receptive to my talk and responded well to questions that I asked, but when I spoke of my mother's death and asked if anyone had seen anything similar, the silence was absolute. However, later that day, an elderly nursing sister came to me and said, 'I know exactly what you meant but I didn't want to speak in front of all those people. Something similar happened many years ago when I was nursing a child who was dying. She did just what you said and I can still remember the radiance of her face and the way she stretched her arms out. Another nurse was with me and she saw it too.'

## Dr Martyn Lloyd-Jones

Dr Martyn Lloyd-Jones, a well-known physician and Welsh Presbyterian minister, described a similar incident to his wife Bethan when he returned to his home in Aberavon after visiting a local character called 'Staffordshire Bill'. He gave this account of the man's death to Bethan, who was herself a doctor:

'He was obviously at perfect peace and all the evidences of the old sinful, violent life were smoothed out of a now child-like face. The minutes passed and became an hour, and more. Then suddenly the painful sound of the difficult breathing seemed to stop. The old man's face was transformed, alight, radiant. He sat up eagerly with up-stretched arms and a beautiful smile on his face, as though welcoming his best of friends, and with that he was gone to that land of pure delight where saints immortal reign.' [17]

Dr Lloyd-Jones was obviously impressed by Bill's death. So what happened to Bill, my mother and the other people whose deaths we have discussed? At her deathbed, I was quite sure that mother had seen something very beautiful, but I do not know what, if anything, she had perceived. When I was with her in the bedroom, two possibilities came to my mind. I thought that she might be greeting my father, or perhaps her own parents, and this would be in line with the findings of Osis and Haraldsson. The other possibility, and the one I tend to favour, is that she had seen

Jesus. My reason for thinking this is based partly on my assessment of her character but mainly on the sense of joy and light that she radiated. It was more than even a well-loved person might have merited.

Early in this section, I said that I had three reasons for being interested in deathbed visions. Two reasons have been mentioned. The third is the paper by Osis and Haraldsson in which, contrary to possible expectations, they showed that deathbed visions are not more common when patients are febrile or have received medical drugs. In fact the reverse is true. They found that the incidence of deathbed visions was reduced by such factors. This is in line with a study I undertook in 1972, which found that people who die at home are less heavily medicated than those who die in hospitals [18] and agrees with my suggestion that deathbed visions are more likely to occur in a domiciliary setting than in other situations. I discussed this possibility with a group of MacMillan nurses in 2005. These nurses specialize in the care of cancer patients at home and most had been present when patients had deathbed visions. The nurses agreed that the visions had occurred only when the patient died at home and not in hospitals. This was their experience, though I do not doubt that deathbed experiences do occur in hospitals, care homes and at the site of accidents; but they are probably less common in those situations.

## You are the Son of God!

A patient's illness can certainly affect their perception of reality. This was highlighted for me in the 1970s, when I was asked to visit an elderly lady who I knew quite well. I diagnosed pneumonia and admitted her to the cottage hospital which was run by the local General Practitioners. Later that day, I visited her and was greeted by the most lovely smile. She took my hand and smothered it with kisses. 'I know who you are,' she said; to which I replied,

'Yes, I know.' Still she held my hand and continued to whisper, 'I know who you are,' and eventually I asked: 'Who do you think I am?' Her reply was quite amazing. 'You are the Son of God,' she said and again kissed my hand. The next day her fever had abated and our relationship resumed its normal pattern.

# CHAPTER 8

# China and Healing

'MUCH OF THE SICKNESS of men and women today is due to a severed or wrong relationship with their ancestors, a relationship with someone 'gone before' which has not been healed.' Early drafts of *Pointers to Eternity* attributed that statement to an Anglican bishop who has since died, but when I checked my references I could not confirm its source and therefore cannot attribute it definitively to a specific person. However, the statement is still likely to surprise the Western mind, because it states so unambiguously that a person's relationship with his/her deceased ancestors can influence their state of health. Admittedly this is not a new idea but one that is normally associated with Asian and African philosophies, yet it has the potential to bring into the Church's ministry of healing ideas that were not acceptable in the past. The amount of credence that the idea merits need not concern us now, but it reminds us that a meeting of different cultures may have an osmotic effect, with the ideas and practices of each being absorbed by the other. In this instance the belief expressed had its origin in China.

The person who opened the issue to debate was Dr Kenneth McAll, founder of the Family Tree Ministry, a Christian approach to healing that is concerned with the resolution of past family traumas. Dr McAll was born in China in 1910, the son of Congregational missionaries, and spent the first nine years of his life in Hankow before being sent to England for his schooling. He went to Eltham College and later to the medical school at

Edinburgh University where he graduated in 1935, before returning to China as a missionary doctor. It was in that capacity that he claimed to have met Jesus whilst walking across an open plain in the late 1930s. It is a story that I heard him tell on a number of occasions, the first time in 1971 when the Presbyterian Church of Wales held its annual Summer School on Healing at Aberystwyth, with Dr McAll as the guest speaker. I was invited to that Summer School. Why, I am not quite sure; possibly because I was a GP in a nearby practice and on the Governing Body of the Church in Wales. I went with some reluctance and did so mainly because I had a high regard for the doctor who had asked me to attend. At that time I was not interested in spiritual healing, I did not want to get involved, and had no desire to hear its merits expounded by a missionary doctor who had been a prisoner of the Japanese. Subsequent events showed that our interests and relationships, though never close, were probably nearer than might have been expected. In the following autumn, I was to publish a paper on bereavement that was relevant to his thesis and some years later I worked alongside his daughter Elizabeth, who had been imprisoned with him by the Japanese. We were also to meet briefly on other occasions.

At our first meeting, Dr McAll asked me to give him a detailed assessment of his talk when it was over. I failed to do so, mainly because the session finished late and I hurried home instead. Also, the content of the talk was so unusual that I needed time to think about it. It was not a particularly well delivered lecture but it was memorable, and when some years later Elizabeth showed me one of his books, I immediately recognized incidents that he had mentioned in Aberystwyth. Hopefully this account will rectify my failure to carry out his wishes in 1971. If it does it will be in keeping with Dr Ken's (as many people called him) philosophy of the need to heal broken or distorted relationships with the deceased.

## Dr McAll returns to China

When Ken McAll returned to China in 1937, his first placement was at a Peking language school where he spent a statutory six months before being appointed superintendent of Siaochang Hospital, an eighty-bed unit in north China. In June 1940 he married Frances, a doctor who had been a fellow medical student in Edinburgh. They began their married life in a region of China that was controlled by the Japanese and was also attracting Chinese partisans of various political factions – most notably the Communists. Siaochang was situated in the north China plain. It was a small town, forty miles from the railway. The road to it was just a cart track across a vast area of millet, a crop that reached a height of over six feet in summer. In winter the ground was bare and frozen. Each year the Yellow River overflowed and flooded the countryside, so most villages were built on slightly elevated ground and possessed at least one boat. The only other transport was by bicycle or mule cart, the latter being so uncomfortable that it was often easier and almost as quick to walk. It was a dangerous area for lone travellers and Dr McAll was sometimes stopped when he visited nearby villages, and there were instances when he was arrested and held for questioning. Once he was brought to trial on a charge of spying and condemned to death by a military court, only to be reprieved because he was a rarity – a surgeon in the area – so he was allowed to carry on with his work.

Siaochang Hospital was unique in that part of China. It was the only centre to provide Western medicine in a region the size of Wales and with a population of ten million people. Its beds were always full and Dr McAll would perform at least twelve major operations a week, as well as helping in the clinics and supervising the running of the hospital and its outlying dispensaries. Part of his work required him to visit local towns and villages, excursions that sometimes meant sleeping rough, walking for days at a time and being harassed by bandits. One evening as the sun was setting, he was walking to a village with medical supplies when a man dressed entirely in white appeared behind him unexpectedly. McAll thought he was a local farmer returning home late, and when the man pointed to a village away from their road and said there were many wounded people in it needing help, he was persuaded to change direction and go to the village. The next part of the story is told by Dr McCall in his book *Healing the Family Tree*:

> 'I went with him to his village. The gates were thrown open and I was pulled inside, but the man was nowhere to be seen. The villagers told me that I had narrowly avoided a Japanese ambush, as the village which had been my destination was now overrun. They questioned me closely about my change of direction and knowledge of their wounded and insisted that no-one from the village had been outside the walls that day. I remembered that the white-robed stranger had spoken to me in English and I was certainly the only foreigner within miles. I knew then that it was Jesus who had appeared to me…and that my daily prayer for protection had been dramatically answered.' [1]

## After Siaochang

This strange encounter had another important consequence which became apparent only after the McAlls had resettled in England. Meanwhile, much else was to happen to them in China. The Japanese now regarded them increasingly as undesirable aliens in a war zone and made them leave Siaochang and settle in Tsinan, the ancient capital of Shantung province. There they worked as medical officers in the university hospital and Frances gave birth to their first child, Elizabeth, in July 1941. Five months later, on 7 December 1941, the Japanese attacked Pearl Harbour and entered World War II as an ally of the Axis powers. This changed the status of the McAll family. They were no longer neutral civilians but enemy aliens and their movements became increasingly restricted. Eventually, they were imprisoned in an internment camp. Conditions in the camps were difficult, but they survived as a family and were able to help people to cope with their health problems. Their release came in August 1945 following the destruction of Hiroshima and Nagasaki, and the McAlls were among the first to be repatriated from China by boat, landing at Southampton on 11 November 1945. They were welcomed by Frances' parents and her sister. [2] By this time they were exhausted in mind and body, each weighing little more than six stone.

Though safely back in the UK, their problems were many. They had no home, no job, few resources and a young daughter to nurture. Kenneth decided to try his hand in general practice in 1947, only a few months before the National Health Service was established. This was not an ideal time to start a new practice; people were reluctant to change doctors once they had selected a GP and he had only 27 registered patients at the beginning of the new scheme. The financial outlook must have looked very bleak. He managed for a while but later decided to take a sideways step and study psychiatry. Subsequently, he established the Family Tree Ministry, the healing ministry which became the focus of his work in later life and which he established in a number of countries before he died.

Readers may reasonably ask: 'What has the Family Tree Ministry to do with Jesus?' The short answer is: 'Everything.' It is probably safe to say that Dr McAll's career would have followed a different path had it not been for his encounter with the mysterious figure on the Chinese plain. The immediate consequences of the meeting were threefold. Firstly, it may have saved his life. We cannot be sure that he would have been killed or injured if he had walked into the ambush that the Japanese had prepared, but it is a possibility and one that the villagers who received him considered likely. Secondly, the wounded men who were sheltering in the village would not have benefited from his surgical skills. Thirdly, it had a profound effect on Kenneth McAll himself. His belief in the power of prayer was reinforced (for instance, that his daily prayer for protection would be answered); and it brought a radical change in his attitude to Chinese customs and beliefs, particularly to the important role the Chinese gave to their continued relationship with the ancestral spirits. Commenting on this later, he said that the intolerance which had characterized his attitude to their beliefs ceased and was replaced by a realization that 'the spirit world holds both good and evil influences'. This change in attitude became the basis for his future work as a psychiatrist, a work in which he was primarily concerned with restoring broken relationships within families, particularly where the underlying problem centred on the dead. It was reconciliation work, and work that he believed Jesus expected him to do 'until the day I die'. [3]

## Feng kuei man

Another incident in China which influenced him greatly was seeing the harsh way that a particular *feng kuei* (devil-mad) man was handled by Chinese peasants. The man had gone berserk and in his madness had been chained to a wall by the villagers who, believing that he was possessed by an evil spirit, set about stoning him to death. He survived the stoning and the villagers, assuming that the man could be cured, sent for an exorcist to drive out the devil. The exorcist was a Bible Christian who had retained the Chinese belief in good and bad spirits. She went to the man, prayed alongside him and offered a prayer of exorcism in the name of Jesus Christ. As she prayed the man slumped unconscious in his chains. This change was accepted by the villagers as a sign that he had been cured, so they cared for him and rehabilitated him.

Ken McAll had observed this with considerable scepticism. He rejected the possibility that the man had been possessed by a spirit and successfully exorcised, but back in England memories of the event continued to trouble him as he thought of the many other people who, like that devil–mad man, needed help. Believing this was the path that God was offering him, he returned to university in 1956 and trained as a psychiatrist.

As a psychiatrist, Dr McAll's approach to people's problems tended to be unorthodox and idiosyncratic. This is not surprising; he had a wide and unusual experience of life, he had lived with people of different cultures and traditions, and his experience of medical practice exceeded that of most doctors. All this was rooted in a firm Christian faith which had been reinforced by his singular meeting with Jesus in north China and the exorcism of the *feng kuei* man. This enabled him to weld together ideas that were based on Christian theology, Chinese philosophy and psychological principles. Because of his long association with the Chinese, he had become aware of the importance of the ancestors to them and the powerful influence they exerted in the life of the nation. But his initial contempt for Chinese beliefs and practices, particularly their on-going respect for their ancestors, changed when Jesus walked with him on the road to the Chinese village. From his training as a psychiatrist he learnt the therapeutic effectiveness of listening, how repression can manifest itself in a wide range of illnesses, and the need to come to terms with the problems of the unconscious mind. His Christian faith brought the realization that inner healing, particularly the healing of memories, comes with acceptance, repentance and forgiveness, and that these virtues are most powerfully expressed when they are associated with the Eucharist, through Christ's sacrifice for the redemption of the world.

## The Family Tree Ministry

Dr McAll made the Eucharist the central rite of the Family Tree Ministry. Its use as a channel of healing is not new, nor is praying for the recently deceased – both are well-established practices in the Roman Catholic and Eastern Orthodox Churches. That these rites should be adopted so ardently by a Scottish Protestant was surprising, for Ken McAll had been raised in a tradition where the Holy Communion service was essentially an act of remembrance and prayers for the dead were anathema. His introduction to the therapeutic possibilities of the Eucharist began in a psychiatric unit where a severely disturbed woman was in a padded cell. Her family was known to the local suffragan bishop, who had been a missionary in Africa and had practised exorcism there. One day the bishop said to Ken, 'Come to me on Saturday and we will have a requiem mass,' – an offer that McAll later admitted, 'made me shiver.' [4] But he went to the mass, during which the patient and her aunt, who was in another mental hospital, were both healed though neither was present in person. It is impossible to gauge the effect, if any, this service had on the women's dead relatives, but the patients were cured and McAll was sufficiently impressed to explore the implications. As a consequence, he began to compile family trees of his patients and to take the issues to the Eucharist. He found the results surprising and worth pursuing and so began the Family Tree Ministry (FTM). McAll's wife, a physician, wrote: 'The FTM exists to promote the Christian healing approach pioneered by Dr McAll. Many mental and some physical diseases may result from past family trauma, e.g. suicide or abortion. Healing follows the committal of the unmourned or unrecognised individual to God.' [5]

As Kenneth McAll developed his ministry he extended it to include wider areas of concern, notably the healing of troubled places and centres of great evil such as concentration camps and battlefields. But his main concern was family relationships, especially any distorted relationship that may exist between the living and the dead, believing that many 'incurable' patients are the victims of ancestral control. He taught that a cure could be effected by identifying the troubled ancestor and releasing the earthbound soul to God's loving care by means of a Eucharist, with family members acting as a proxy for the deceased when receiving the sacraments. In doing this, he always stressed the necessity never to seek to make contact with the dead in any way, including praying to them.

## Freud and Jung

Although Dr McAll was profoundly influenced by traditional Chinese beliefs, his *Weltanschauung* (philosophy of life) was widened by the teachings of Sigmund Freud and Carl Jung. Like most English psychiatrists, he did not identify particularly closely with either tradition, both of which speak of the 'unconscious' mind – Freud in terms of the personal unconscious and Jung giving greater weight to the collective unconscious. Freud formulated the idea of 'repression' – as the tendency of the ego to hide within the unconscious, experiences, thoughts and feelings that are too distressing for the conscious mind to handle. This is in line with the observation that many families have black sheep and skeletons in the cupboard which are considered 'best forgotten' and tend not to be mentioned publicly. They may be criminals or drug addicts, stillborn children or aborted babies – innocent lives that were destroyed and remain unacknowledged, yet not entirely forgotten. McAll believed that these individuals survive as lost souls who need to be helped, partly for their own sake but also because their wraith-like existence damages the well-being of surviving friends and relatives. The continued impact of these forgotten people on the lives of the living was an aspect of Chinese teaching that became acceptable to Dr McAll after his meeting with Jesus. In seeking to help them, he found that the most effective method was through the Eucharist. This approach was quite revolutionary, as Western medicine has always been concerned with the living only, and not at all with the dead.

## The healing Eucharist

The central act of the Family Tree Ministry is the Eucharist. Preparation for the service is of particular importance and the people who wish to attend begin by constructing a family tree and identifying those for whom healing prayers are needed. These individuals may include the living and the dead, but a special emphasis is placed on the needs of the deceased, on babies who were aborted, miscarried or stillborn, on people who had committed suicide or died in emotional distress or in some violent way. During this service, babies are referred to by name so that the prayer becomes specific and personal, but if they had never been given a name this should now be done. The sorrows and pain associated with the deceased should be spoken aloud during the service and forgiveness and regrets clearly expressed.

The structure of the service is similar to most Eucharistic Services but tends to focus on the needs of the family. The intention of the prayers is almost entirely for the deceased and each person is named individually. Another variant is that unlimited time is allowed for each person present to read out any confession and prayers they have written and brought to the service. These prayers are not offered sequentially but are spoken by those present simultaneously, producing a remarkable murmur of sound within the congregation. When the sacrament is taken, this is received in part for oneself but mainly for those being remembered. The service may be public or private, but it always ends with a blessing and the focus then shifts from the needs of the dead to those of the living.

## Maori Tangi

The Family Tree Ministry contains elements that exist in the Maori culture, particularly in a Maori *Tangi,* or funeral. At a *Tangi* the recently dead are released into the care of the long dead, and the survivors are reminded that those who have died will continue to influence them by their spiritual presence. Maori traditions teach that the lives of the living and deceased are closely intertwined and that the deceased continue to share in the everyday life of the living. It is an intercommunion between the living and the dead that acquired a greater reality to Gerard Hughes, a Jesuit priest, when he was on a pilgrimage to Jerusalem in 1987.

On one day of the pilgrimage, whilst he was walking through Germany, Gerald Hughes' thoughts turned to members of his family who had died, and he found himself talking to them. That night he lodged in a widow's house and during the evening meal she told him about her husband who had died twenty years previously. Even after all that time she still sensed her husband's presence, spoke to him frequently and drew great strength and comfort from doing so. She had not dared to tell her family or friends about this, in case they thought her mad. Of his own and the widow's experiences, Gerald Hughes wrote:

> 'I have met many other people who have had this same experience, which feels perfectly natural, comforting, reassuring and in no way spooky. The dead are like shy guests at a party: they will not intrude and can easily go unnoticed. If, however, we give them attention, we can become increasingly aware of their comforting presence. Those who have died remain alive in the God in whom all creation has its being. It would seem to follow that they will be in contact with us in some way.' [6]

One cannot say what benefits Gerald Hughes obtained from his pilgrimage, but it is apparent that during his walk through Germany he gained a deeper insight into the relationships that can exist between the living and the dead. It is in the nurturing of such relationships that Western practices differ so markedly from the traditional practices of the Maori, the Chinese and many African tribes.

## Cultural significance

The cultural significance of Kenneth McAll's meeting with the risen Christ is potentially great. Before discussing its possible implications, one needs to consider the structure of Chinese society at that time.

In the 1930s, Chinese society was firmly based on the Confucian principles that had regulated the country for over 2,000 years. The father was head of the household, and this functioned within the spirit of reciprocity – a code of mutual responsibility between parents and a son that was central to the family's ability to operate as a strong and continuing unit. When the son was young, he was cared for and nurtured by his parents; as he grew older he assumed increasing responsibility within the family, and in his turn he cared for his parents when they became old and incapable. Similarly, daughters would provide for their parents-in-law in return for the care that they had received from their parents. Such reciprocal care within the family environment is commonplace throughout the world, but the Chinese situation differed from that in the West because in China the caring relationship was maintained after the death of the parents. Dr Hugh Baker, of the University of London School of Oriental and African Studies, had this to say about the relationships: 'Death did not release the son from his duty to his parents, it merely altered the form which his duty took. While alive, parents were served and respected; dead they were served and worshipped. In return the ancestors gave to their descendants such blessings and assistance as were in their supernatural power.' [7]

It was Dr McAll's acceptance of this continued interaction between the living and the dead that enabled him to establish a new ministry of healing within a Christian context. There are, of course, important differences in this relationship from those practised in the East. The Chinese and Japanese custom is to provide food and other offerings at the altar consecrated to the ancestors. In contrast, McAll's ministry is centred upon the Eucharist, in which Christ's sacrificial offering is received by family members on behalf of the deceased. By accepting the validity of the Chinese belief in the omnipresence of ancestral spirits, Dr McAll has, perhaps inadvertently, enabled the Christian doctrine of the Resurrection to be placed more firmly within the cultural tradition of oriental peoples. If a sceptical Western missionary can acknowledge the reality of the continuing involvement of the spirits of the dead in everyday affairs, then it seems likely that Eastern peoples may find it easier to embrace Christian beliefs into their own traditions. This is also true in Africa, where people of many nationalities venerate their dead forebears. They share the belief that much of the sickness in the world today is the result of flawed relationships with the dead and they recognize a need to re-establish good relationships with family members who have died unmourned and unforgiven.

People are more mobile now than formerly. Some travel for pleasure, others to find a livelihood, but constant relocation can create a sense of being rootless and of having no reason to live. The search for a meaning to life is universal, and for many people this search may be aided if the experiences they have of their dead loved ones can be associated more closely with the Christian message of forgiveness and Resurrection. Through his meeting with Jesus, Ken McAll has helped to bring these two aspects of life closer together. In Jungian terms, the ministry he established may be seen as a waterfall that unites different, though similar, streams of ideas and beliefs. These ideas are all centred on the reality of an afterlife. Following McAll's death, the FTM ceased to exist as an international venture but his books have been translated into a dozen languages and his ideas widely disseminated. A resource document, *Praying for the Family Tree*, is available from a former associate. [8]

It is possible that Dr McAll's ideas will fade away and his insights lost. This would be a pity but there are precedents to suggest it might happen. Early Jesuit missionaries to China allowed converts to incorporate into their newfound Christian beliefs practices that were akin to ancestor worship. These so-called 'Chinese rites' were condemned by Pope Clement X1 in 1715 and Pope Benedict X1V in 1742, and were disallowed. [9] The circumstances are different now. The ancient civilizations of China, Japan and many other countries are recognized as having much to offer the modern world both materially and spiritually, and in the West our understanding of the needs of the bereaved have changed greatly.

## China and Emmaus

Ken McAll's encounter on a track in China bears a close resemblance to Jesus' meeting with the men on the road to Emmaus. The following points of similarity are worth noting:

1  On both occasions the meetings occurred towards evening as the sun was setting.

2  Jesus appeared unexpectedly.

3  He walked with them and talked to them.

4  The content of his speech was relevant to the situation.

5  They did not recognize him immediately.

6  He left them suddenly – he just seemed to vanish.

7  They recognized him only at the point of departure (after the

breaking of bread at Emmaus and after McAll was dragged through the village gate).

8   The meeting had a profound effect on the lives of those involved.

# CHAPTER 9

# Other Cultures

IN THEIR REPLY TO my letter, some bishops asked if our knowledge of Christic visions was limited to educated Anglo-Saxon Christians. They wanted to know if research had been done into the experiences of people from a wider cultural and educational background. Apart from Weibe's book and the study by Osis and Haraldsson which have been mentioned already, I know of no such research; but this chapter does offer instances of other meetings with Jesus that I have chanced upon and consider worth recording. Of the four people reported in this chapter, each came from a different ethnic group and none was a Christian when they had their encounter with Jesus.

## The prisoner

I learnt of Fred Lemon when I was a counsellor at a nearby Young Offender's Institute. My access to the prison was facilitated by its chaplain. Although prisons are sometimes likened to monasteries, the difference is enormous. Prisons, for instance, are noisy institutions whilst monasteries are quiet places, and the culture and attitudes within a prison differs greatly from that outside the walls. This is true for prisoners and prison officers alike.

When Dr McAll met Jesus, they walked together across open country in China. In contrast, Fred Lemon met him in one of England's bleakest prisons, HMP Dartmoor, on the night of 10 August 1950. He was alone in a cell, serving a two-year sentence for robbery with violence, and was getting a particularly hard time from the prison officers, not because of his criminal record but because he was showing an unusual interest in religion. He had visited the prison chapel and then started to read the Bible and pray each day, but his motives for doing so were regarded as suspicious; consequently he was dealt with particularly stringently. Fred rebelled and was charged with misconduct. He was found guilty and sentenced to a period in solitary confinement with loss of privileges.

When Fred was released from solitary and returned to his own cell, he was a very angry man who was determined to exact vengeance and injure an officer nicknamed 'Tojo'. After the cell door was locked behind him, he lay on his bunk and nursed his grievances. Eventually he dropped off into a fitful doze, then woke up suddenly to find three men standing beside him. They were not prison warders or policemen but ordinary-looking men wearing civilian suits. One man pointed to the man in the middle and said, 'Fred, this is Jesus.' The man in the middle stood there and talked to Fred. He knew everything about his past life, recounting it in detail and telling him how he was to behave in future. While this was happening, Fred sat on the edge of the bed with his head in his hands, staring at the floor and listening to what the man was saying. The downward cast of his eyes may explain why he never saw the faces of the men standing in front of him. He could see their clothes and that these were immaculately pressed but their faces were not clear.

At the time, Fred had no sense of fear or awe. He just felt a wonderful certainty that 'through this man Jesus, God was offering me forgiveness – had in fact already forgiven my sins'. [1] He did not remember the exact words that were spoken, only that Jesus said quite clearly that if Fred wanted to be a Christian then he had to 'drive the hatred from his heart'. The three men disappeared quietly. They simply faded through the wall facing Fred all the time, then he heard a click and he was alone. He felt an enormous sense of peacefulness, lay down and slept like a child. When he awoke in the morning, he remembered the experience so clearly that he knew it could not have been a dream. This insight was not reassuring; instead he became suddenly confused and anxious. Fearing that he might be going mad, he decided to tell no-one until the Methodist chaplain returned from his holiday, because the Reverend Percy Holmes was the only person he could trust to tell of this meeting with Jesus.

Before the chaplain returned from holiday, Fred began to practise the advise that Jesus had given him, and was emptying his heart of all anger, bitterness and hatred towards others. This inner change became so noticeable in its effect on others that the warders also changed their assessment and attitude to him. Fred's change in attitude is recorded clearly in the Foreword to his autobiography, where the Secretary of the Christian Police Association says of Fred that 'he is living evidence that Christ makes all things new'. [2] The story is most unusual as it tells of Jesus visiting a man in prison. Nothing similar is recorded in the New Testament, though Philip Weibe does record a similar episode in *Visions of Jesus* where he reports the story of Ernie Hollands.

## The Japanese lady

I learnt of this vision during a visit to the Syrian Orthodox Cathedral in Jerusalem in May 2005. I was with a group of people that Canon Andrew White was taking around the Holy Land and we were in a chapel beneath the main body of St Mark's Cathedral listening to Ustina, the church guide. Andrew had explained already that this chapel was the most likely site (among the possible contenders) for the Upper Room where Jesus held his last Passover meal and had inaugurated the Eucharistic feast that is celebrated by Christians.

Ustina was recounting the historical and spiritual associations of the place, when she suddenly digressed and started to tell us about a Japanese lady whom she had met in the chapel. The lady had had visions of Jesus for the past three years, and in the visions she was told to go to Jerusalem and visit the Upper Room where she would meet a woman called Ustina. Despite the antipathy of her family, she made the journey to Jerusalem, came to the chapel and knelt down in prayer. As she prayed, her eyes filled with tears and she began to cry; this was observed by Ustina who was standing nearby. When the woman became calmer, Ustina spoke to her and learnt of the events that had brought her to the chapel, and that she had seen Jesus again whilst praying in the chapel. Both women were very moved by their meeting and when Ustina revealed her identity, there were more tears and much embracing.

It would have been good to have got a more detailed account of the visions seen by the Japanese lady. I wanted to know if Jesus had appeared as a physical presence, what language he spoke, whether she had heard him speak with her physical ears or as an inward voice, and how she knew it was Jesus; but there was no way that these uncertainties could be explored further. We were told, however, that the Japanese lady became a Christian and that some months later she returned with her boyfriend who also became a Christian. They were married in St Mark's in the presence of Canon Andrew White, who verified the general truth of the story as did his Palestinian aide, Hanna. (We were told that Hanna's father had a prominent role in the marriage service, as he gave the bride away.)

## The Muslim

The Japanese lady's vision of Jesus had a good outcome. She married her lover and they both became Christians. From a social perspective, the Muslim gentleman fared less well. I learnt about him from Dr Christopher Lamb, Canon Theologian at Coventry Cathedral and a former missionary in Pakistan. When asked if he knew any Muslims who had seen Jesus, Christopher reflected for a moment and said he did know one such man and told me the following story.

The Muslim was a member of a powerful Pakistani family with extensive business connections. He had been sent to London to oversee the family concerns in the UK. Everything seemed perfect: he was rich, successful, and happy in the life he lived with his wife and children, until he had a vision of the crucified Jesus. It occurred whilst he was standing in his garden in London, and the words that came to him from the vision – whether spoken aloud or heard silently within is not known – were: 'See how I have suffered for you'. Jesus did not appear as a man standing on the ground but as a vision in the sky, and the Muslim knew that the pattern of his life would be changed. At the time he had no close contact with Christians but he started to seek them out and became a Christian. Then his life fell apart. His family disowned him and he lost his position within the business. His wife divorced him because a Muslim woman cannot be married to a Christian. In effect he lost everything but, despite the losses, the man had no sense of resentment at the way he was treated by those who were closest to him. He had chosen to follow Jesus and had responded to the words that came from the vision. That Jesus appeared in his crucified form to the man and that the latter accepted the reality of the vision is remarkable, because as a Muslim he would have been taught, probably from an early age, that Jesus did not die on the cross.

## The Sikh

The incidents mentioned so far in this chapter concern people who are or were contemporaries of mine, yet who are mostly unknown. Sundhar Singh was different. He died in 1929 but his name is fresh in the memory of many people in North India and during his life he was well known in Europe as a missionary and man of God. He is commemorated in the Anglican Book of Offices *Celebrating Common Prayer* where he is described as 'an Evangelist, Teacher and Sadhu'. [3] Details of his life can be found on the website where I was able to refresh my own recollections of this remarkable man.

Born in 1889 in the Punjab, Sundhar Singh was the son of an affluent Sikh family. In his early teens, he was devastated by the death of a brother and his mother and probably as a consequence of these bereavements became very interested in the significance and purpose of life. By the age of 16, he knew the *Bhagavad-Gita* by heart and had read other major religious texts including the Bible, the *Guru Granth Sahib*, the *Qur'an* and most of the *Upanishads*, but from these he got no adequate explanation for the enigma of life. One day, in a fit of despair he took his school's copy of the Christian Gospels and burnt it publicly. This act gave no relief and he then prayed to God asking for a sign that would end his doubts and misery, vowing that if this was not granted he would kill himself. That night he had a vision of Jesus who spoke in Hindustani and asked, 'How long will you persecute me? I have come to save you; you were praying to know the right way. Why do you not take it?' He responded by falling at Jesus' feet. Then he went into his father's bedroom, awoke him and told him what had happened. [4]

On reaching adult status in 1904, he had his hair cut and was expelled from his father's house and from the Sikh community. A month later he took the vow of a Sadhu, donned the saffron robe of an ascetic mendicant and became a barefoot evangelist for

Christ, travelling into Tibet and making a leper hospital his base when in the Punjab. In 1909, he entered the Anglican College in Lahore with the intention of studying for the ministry, but rejected the opportunities this offered when he learnt that he would be expected to discard the saffron robe of a Sadhu and adopt the lifestyle of an Anglican clergyman. The stories about him are legendary. He had many mystical visions of Jesus and of these he wrote: 'Christ on his throne is always in the centre, a figure ineffable and indescribable. The face as I see it in ecstasy with my spiritual eyes, is very much the same as I saw it at my conversion with my bodily eyes. He has scars with blood flowing from them. The scars are not ugly but glowing and beautiful... The hair on his head is like gold, like glowing light. The face is like the sun, but it is light that does not dazzle me.' In assessing the visions he wrote: 'I have had visions and I know how to distinguish them. But I have seen Jesus only once.'

The account Sundhar Singh gives of his visions is noteworthy, though much is left unsaid. At his conversion he saw Jesus with his 'bodily eyes', not as on subsequent occasions with his 'spiritual eyes'. This suggests, though we cannot be sure, that Jesus appeared to him in a physical form as happened at the Resurrection. He also spoke in Hindustani, though whether Sundhar Singh heard the words with his inner hearing or his physical hearing is not stated. We know nothing of the garments Jesus wore but we are given some insight into his facial appearance. It was the overwhelming grandeur of the face that impressed and we are not surprised that details of lesser significance – whether it was an Arabic, Asian or Caucasian face – are omitted. For the teenage youth, the important factor was that the person he saw was Jesus Christ. His initial encounter, however we choose to interpret it, was a life-changing event and one that had a considerable impact on many people including his father, who also became a Christian.

## Comparative experiences

When Jesus appeared to his disciples at the Resurrection, he did so suddenly and unexpectedly. He appeared to them in this way outside the tomb, in a closed room, on the road to Emmaus and when they were fishing. The Gospel accounts indicate that his departures tended to be similarly abrupt. This pattern is reflected in the reports we have of more recent encounters: his appearing to Fred Lemon in a prison cell, to Dr McAll on the Chinese plain and to Donald English in his wife's bedroom. In these three instances, he appeared as a solid figure and communicated with them in English. Other instances are not quite the same but the language spoken always seemed appropriate. Two thousand years ago when Jesus spoke to Saul outside Damascus it was in the Jewish tongue; more recently he spoke to Sundhar Singh in Hindustani, but we don't always know the language used or how it was perceived. Donald English and Bishop Montefiore both said that they heard the voice within themselves and there was no external sound. This manner of communication has a biblical pedigree dating back to Abram (Genesis 15) and Elijah (1 Kings 19: 13). From a medical perspective, an inner voice is less likely to point to a hallucinatory/psychotic experience than one that is considered to come from outside the body. We assume that in his Resurrection appearances Jesus communicated with his disciples in a normal conversational manner, and there is no reason to doubt that this was so, but it does seem that in his post-Ascension encounters he does vary his mode of communication.

The experiences some people have of Jesus are best described as visionary, but this is not always the case; some people do see him as a solid figure who is instantly recognizable as Jesus. In contrast, at the Easter appearances he was not always recognized by people who knew him well, and on one occasion he was mistaken for a ghost. The reasons for these discrepancies require an explanation which, regretfully, I cannot give.

At his Resurrection, Jesus was seen as a person of normal height and general appearance, and his behaviour was appropriate for the circumstances in which he appeared. This was the way that some of my contemporaries perceived him, but whilst Donald English and Kenneth McAll *inter al.* saw him as a person and heard him speak, neither mentioned being touched by him. That is not surprising as their accounts are brief and the salient facts are provided, but the Gospels do give at least one instance of physical contact. Similarly, as we shall see in the next chapter, widowed people do occasionally report being touched, but the incidence of such contact is small compared with other perceptions of the deceased. However, Philip Weibe in his book *Visions of Jesus* says that when Ernie Hollands was standing in his prison cell, the 'door opened up, Jesus walked through it towards Ernie, stood in front of him, touched him on his left shoulder (which he felt) and said three things'. [5] These words, which were of great importance to Ernie, did not appear to come from the lips of Jesus, but it seemed 'as though it was thunder coming from inside'. Similarly, the writer of Letter 2 in Chapter 6 says of her experience that 'most powerfully of all was His Presence and His voice'. So the character of the voice can vary. The words may come from the lips of Jesus or it may be an inner voice, sometimes described as a still small voice or like thunder. This is one way that the post-Ascension experiences differ from the Easter appearances, for in the latter he always spoke in a normal conversational voice.

Another feature distinguishes the Gospel narratives from more recent reports. Only in the Gospels do we learn that the resurrected Jesus sat down and shared food with his followers. This was a crucial, indeed foundational, moment in the life of the Church. He had allowed men to see him, speak with him and touch him, and had reproached them for their incredulity and dullness, but this was the only occasion in the history of the . Church when people were allowed to share food in a normal manner with the risen Jesus. Forever afterwards, this sustenance could only be received in the sacrament of the Eucharist, the food of Holy Communion.

# Section 4

# The Widowed

CHAPTER 10

# Widows' Tales

IN HIS BOOK *EASTER Faith,* Gerald O'Collins refers to a study on widows and widowers that I published in 1971. His comments are kind and generous but his assessment of the relevance of the findings to our understanding of the Resurrection differs from mine. Consequently, it seems proper for me to give an account of that study – why it was undertaken, the results that were obtained and the importance that I think should be ascribed to them. Hopefully this will enable discussions on the Resurrection to engage a wider audience than the relatively few theologians who are mainly concerned with it at present. After all, the Resurrection is of importance to everyone and whilst the historical evidence is limited to a few pages in the New Testament, its reality is confirmed for millions of people through what they consider to be personal contact with their deceased relatives. By this means they have an experiential justification for accepting as true the Easter message that Christ is Risen. It does not replace the biblical and theological bases for the Christian belief, it merely complements them.

My study on widows was undertaken in the aftermath of World War II, when there was a keen interest in matters relating to death and bereavement. New groups, such as Cruse and the Compassionate Friends, were being established to support the bereaved, and books and learned papers flowed from the pens of psychiatrists and thanatologists. Names like Elizabeth Kubler-Ross, Raymond Moody, John Bowlby, Murray Parkes and

Kenneth Ring had become familiar to a wide circle of people. D Scott Rogo was another researcher involved in this work and in 1986 he offered the following comment on our developing insight into bereaved people's experiences of their dead loved ones. Referring to the growing evidence that contact with the dead is surprisingly common, he wrote:

'Psychologists first made this discovery in the early 1970s when they began studying the psychology of death and the mourning process. Dr W Dewi Rees published the first major study in 1971 when he reported on 'the hallucinations of widowhood' in the *British Medical Journal*. It was an eye-opener. Rees polled 293 widows and widowers about their experiences following the death of a spouse and found that close to half of them (47%) believed that they had been in momentary contact with them since that time. These contacts not only came immediately after the deaths, Rees learned, but sometimes even many years later. Some of the meetings were fleeting telepathic interactions, while others were fully fledged apparitional experiences. Obviously a new psychological (?) dimension to the mourning process was being uncovered. When the Rees findings were made known, researchers at Wayne State University were so intrigued that they decided to replicate the study. They obtained very similar results.' [1]

## The Llanidloes Study of Widowhood

A detailed account of the survey has been reported elsewhere [2,3,4] – but some basic facts may help the reader. The study was overseen by a senior psychiatrist appointed by the University of London. He brought three other psychiatrists into the supervisory role: two were professors and the third was an expert in bereavement studies. The statistical data was analysed by Sylvia Lutkins, a research worker at the Department of Mathematics at Aberystwyth University.

My involvement with the project was almost accidental. At the time I was a family doctor at Llanidloes, a small town in rural Wales, and had already published a paper entitled *The Mortality of Bereavement* in association with Sylvia Lutkins. The paper had been well received and I was planning to undertake a detailed study on the medical problems associated with bereavement. During the pilot survey, I spoke to many bereaved people including teenagers and the very old, and was struck by the frequency with which the widowed spoke of their continued relationships with their dead spouses. Often this was just a sense of the person being present nearby, but sometimes it was more explicit and they would speak of occasions when they would see their dead partner, always looking well and happy, or hear them speak.

These disclosures by the bereaved were totally unexpected. I had never encountered anything like them previously and I soon realized that they had not been revealed to my partners or the local clergy, or in most instances to any other person. A survey of the medical literature revealed a remarkable lack of information on the subject. It was not mentioned in the textbooks on psychiatry and no attempt had been made to assess the frequency of these events. We did not even know whether they should be viewed as a wish fulfilment, a form of psychosis, or a normal outcome of bereavement in perfectly sane people.

These preliminary findings were so interesting that I decided to discontinue the planned study on morbidity in order to focus the research on widowed people and determine the frequency and nature of the experiences that they were disclosing to me. The field work was undertaken in a well defined area of mid-Wales where all the residents were patients of the practice. For the study, 295 widowed people were contacted with only two refusing to co-operate, a remarkably high success rate (over 99%) for any medico-social survey. Of the 293 widowed people interviewed, 227 were widows and 66 were widowers. Of these,

48.8% reported having had some perception of, or contact with, their dead spouse following the bereavement, and 36.1% said that this awareness of the dead spouse remained an ongoing process. In each case, their awareness of the presence of the dead spouse occurred in clear consciousness and was never sought. It was always spontaneous and, most importantly, no spiritual medium was ever involved in the process.

This outcome was surprising. I found myself drawn involuntarily into an area that crossed the boundaries between psychology and parapsychology, and one where it was eventually impossible not to consider the religious implications of what my patients had told me. And it all happened in a quiet, rural part of Wales. One important and unexpected result was due entirely to the statistical analyses of Sylvia Lutkins. She showed that although the study was undertaken in a well-defined area of mid-Wales, the findings were relevant not just to local people but to the UK as a whole. Later studies in the US and elsewhere replicated the Llanidloes study and findings.

Whilst most subsequent studies followed the Llanidloes pattern, others included data on people's dreams of the deceased. This introduces a variant that alters the nature of the survey as I had decided not to include dreams and only to record events that had occurred when the individual was wide awake and fully conscious. Also, none of my interviewees had tried to contact the dead; all their experiences had occurred spontaneously. All were interviewed in a one-to-one and face-to-face situation, usually in their own homes. Postal questionnaires and other forms of communication were not used.

The widowed perceived the presence of the dead in different ways. Most commonly there was 'a sense of the presence of the dead spouse' which was reported by 39.2% of those interviewed. This experience was sometimes a fleeting, one-off event but more usually it was a recurrent phenomenon that continued for many years. Visual (14 %), auditory (11.6 %) and tactile (2.7 %) perceptions of the dead spouse were reported as well. In other words many widowed people had, and continue to have, instances when they are aware of the presence of their dead spouse. Some also see them, hear them and even occasionally feel their touch. Most widowed people (69%) find the encounters helpful and pleasant. Only a few (6%) considered them unpleasant, a response that was most likely to be reported when touched.

In planning the survey, the likelihood that peoples' perceptions of the deceased would vary with socio-economic status was considered and looked for. The statistical analysis of the data showed a remarkable consistency in the incidence of these encounters when they were tested against a range of sociological markers. Thus in addition to the frequency being the same for widows and widowers, the incidence was not affected by age of widowhood, cultural background, personality type, religious practice or place of residence (i.e. in a city, town, village or isolated residence) at the time of bereavement. Social isolation and loneliness did not affect the incidence, nor did any previously recorded mental or emotional illness. The perceptions were less frequent when the marriage was said to be unhappy, and more common among the 'professional and managerial class' than other social groups.

The statistical analysis showed that the incidence did not vary with the geographical area in which the death had taken place. This absence of variation was absolute. In other words the incidence remained completely constant wherever the deaths occurred, whether this was in the practice area, elsewhere in Wales or outside Wales.

Overall, the main findings of the survey were as follows:

1) Perceptions of the deceased spouse are normal experiences in widowhood.

2) They are common, occurring in almost 50 per cent of widowed people.

3) They occur irrespective of sex, race domicile, and cultural or religious background.

4) Most percipients find them helpful.

5) They do not affect overt behaviour.

6) They tend to disappear with time.

7) There is no evidence of associated mental illness to suggest they are abnormal.

8) People are able to integrate the experience and keep it secret.

9) Not having such experiences is also common and normal.

## Confirmatory reports

The study received wide coverage in the national and medical press when it was published in the *British Medical Journal* in 1971. Not surprisingly, other researchers undertook their own surveys to see if the results could be refuted. In fact the opposite finding occurred. Subsequent reports confirmed the Llanidloes findings, and some of these reports will be mentioned here. In Iceland, Haraldsson [5] found that about half of the widows and widowers he contacted had experiences of their dead spouse and similar results were reported by Greeley [6] in the US and by Glick and his colleagues in Boston. [7] Glick's team had not expected to encounter the phenomenon, but they found that 47% of young widows experienced the feeling that 'my husband watches over me' even though the women knew their husbands were dead. Data provided by the Harvard child bereavement study showed that orphaned children can feel the same way about their dead parent [8] and that over 70% believe that the deceased parent is watching over them. The children included in the Harvard study were aged between 6 and 17 years.

In North Carolina, Olson and his colleagues interviewed 46 widows living in nursing homes and found that 61% were aware of the presence of their dead spouse. Most considered this to be good or helpful, most had not mentioned it to anyone previously and 46% continued to feel that their dead husband was still with them. The authors said that the results were surprisingly similar to those of the Llanidloes survey and showed that these experiences are more common in the US than is generally recognized. They also pointed out that the studies so far published showed a remarkable agreement in the percentage of the bereaved who have a perception of their dead loved ones. They considered that these facts were not widely known to the medical community or to the population at large, and suggested that a new nomenclature was needed to remove the stigma associated with the word 'hallucination' from these experiences. [9] I agree fully with this last statement. I have always realized that the term 'hallucination' is inappropriate (as is 'pseudo-hallucination' which is sometimes used by psychiatrists) but I could think of no better word to use then and have not been able to coin an acceptable alternative subsequently.

## The widowed speak

Statistical data are useful but they can be very dull. Statistics are a mathematical tool that deal with basic facts and underlying patterns, but viewed from the outside their content can resemble a skeleton that is devoid of living tissue. This section seeks to enlarge our understanding of the statistics by allowing the widowed to recount their experiences in their own words. Please remember that each person was interviewed at length and that only their more salient phrases are recorded here. The duration of widowhood is shown in brackets after the verbatim report.

*A sense of the presence*

This the most common (39.2%) of the experiences reported.

> I feel he is always in the house. It is right pleasant. (1 year)
>
> He is always with me. (2 years)
>
> I feel he is watching me. (2 years)
>
> She did come last week. She was there in spirit. I was surprised. (3 years)
>
> Very often he is by my side. It is a funny thing, I've never dreamt of him. (4 years)
>
> He seems so close. (7 years)
>
> He's there with me now. I am not a bit nervous or miserable. Whenever I am out, I want to go home because he is there. I slept from the first night that he was buried. (8 years)
>
> I know she is with me, when I speak to her she goes away. (9 years)
>
> I felt for one week about two years ago that he was with me all the time. I was not afraid of it. (10 years)
>
> There's nothing like it. It's worth more than all the money in the world to me. It's a lovely feeling. I am very happy, I never feel alone. (10 years)
>
> It stops me doing things that I might otherwise do – like drinking. (14 years)

Some respondents said that this 'sense of the presence' (SOP) had a continuing effect on their lives. For instance, four widows declined an opportunity to remarry because they felt that their deceased spouse was opposed to it; one widow even broke off an engagement for this reason. Perhaps surprisingly, remarriage does not seem to affect the incidence of this sense. Of the 26 people who married again, eleven felt the continued presence of the dead spouse and, in some instances, this experience continued well into the second marriage. Moreover, the new spouse was usually not aware of this continued relationship.

*A sense of protection*

Ten widows said that they felt guided and protected by their dead spouse. In contrast, only one widower said that he felt supported in a similar manner. He was a senior naval officer who believed that his wife had found him his new home. The sense of protection and loss of fear associated with widowhood brings to mind the guiding and protective function of angels recorded in the Bible and elsewhere. The widows' comments are listed below, and it is worth noting that this sense of being protected can persist for a long time.

> I ask his advice on everything. (1 year)
>
> I feel many times that there is some guidance. (4 years)
>
> I feel safer alone in the house now than before he died. (2 years)
>
> I don't feel a bit afraid, he is with me all the time. It's beautiful. (4 years)
>
> If something crops up, I feel him very close and I am guided by him. (5 years)
>
> I feel that no harm can come to me because he is always around me. (6 years)
>
> I feel that he is with me and looking after me. (11 years)
>
> I feel him guiding me. (15 years)
>
> I feel he is helping me still. (26 years)

*Visual perceptions*

> I have only seen him once. He was passing through the gate. He looked very happy. I didn't have a chance to speak to him. (4 years)
>
> He was very plain to me, I was about my work in the house. He disappeared when I was about to speak to him. (10 years)
>
> I have shaken hands with her once or twice, I thought it very nice to see her. (11 years)
>
> She's always wearing the same clothes. (20 years)

*Hearing the deceased*

> I am not lonely because he is with me all the time. I hear him saying, 'I'm alright, Mary.' I am very happy. (6 months)

> I hear him say, 'Don't worry.' (6 months)

> I fancy if I left here I would be running away from him. Lots of people wanted me to go but I just couldn't. He speaks quite plainly. He looks younger, just as he was when he was alright, never as he was ill. (9 months)

> When I heard his voice I would think, 'Why, he's alive,' and then I would think, 'No, it can't be, he is dead.' It upset me very much, it wasn't right. (5 years)

> I think she got me my present house. I find hearing her breathing disturbing but I like the feeling she is in the house. (16 years)

> Whenever I am troubled he seems to say, 'Keep a stiff upper lip'. (12 years)

The last statement was provided by a widow whose husband had left her for another woman 10 years before he died. She then moved from Kent to Wales. She had no experience of her husband whilst he was alive, only after he died.

*Talking to the deceased*

Surviving spouses sometimes speak to their beloved dead. This conversation may be associated with an SOP but in many cases there is no sense of the dead person being present. However, if a widowed person attempts to speak to a spouse whom they can see, the vision is not likely to persist.

> I talk to her especially in the car. I talk to her for hours in the car. When I am chatting to her I am content. I prefer to be alone on a journey. (2 years)

> I talked to her once as I was going to bed. They were very appropriate words. Her voice was as plain as ever. (7 years)

> I often wonder why he doesn't answer me when I speak, but he is dead of course. (10 years)

After I have had a chat I feel better. (10 years – this widow had remarried)

I often have a chat with him, that's why I've never bothered with anyone else. (27 years)

## Being touched

Touch was the least frequent experience. It was reported by only 2.7% of widowed people and was the form of contact that was most often described as disturbing or even frightening. Paradoxically, its use may have been the most pertinent demonstration of the reality of Christ's Resurrection, because it was by the breaking of bread and by eating in the presence of the disciples that the risen Jesus chose to manifest himself most distinctly to his followers.

I have felt him touch my shoulder.

On one occasion in the afternoon soon after he died, I definitely felt his presence and he kissed my face.

I very often feel he is in bed with me. I pull the clothes over me and think that's silly. (2 years)

Only once when I was in bed, he put his arm on me, I was frightened. (5 years)

I felt him touch me, it frightened me, made you think you were going up the wall. (8 years)

On one occasion he touched me on the shoulder when I was standing at the sink. I have heard him breathing during the night and calling me during the day. He was ill for many years and had terrible nights. It was so hard for me and he used to accuse me of going out with other men. When I die I want to be cremated and my ashes put in his grave. I feel closer to him than to Edmund. I married Edmund for company, there's no-one like your first love. (22 years)

## Reasons given for not disclosing the experiences

In the 1960s when I carried out the field work, most of the people (72.3%) had not discussed their experience with anyone else. No doctor had been informed and only one person had mentioned it to a clergyman who was a minister in the English Presbyterian Church. When I discussed the findings with the local Catholic priest, he was not surprised. 'I would be the last person they would tell,' was his comment. Among the other local clergy, some were obviously interested in hearing about the study, others were not. However, attitudes change and people are more willing to discuss these issues now and clergy are more aware of their existence than formerly. Here are some reasons that widowed people gave in the 1960s for keeping their experiences secret.

> They would think it most queer. (9 months)
>
> I don't think anyone has any business with my feelings, that's my business. (2 years)
>
> No-one else has asked me. (3 years)
>
> People only make fun of you; the less you tell people the better. (3 years)
>
> I do not speak of it to anyone else. They do not understand, very few people understand. (8 years)
>
> They would think I was silly. It does seem silly after 9 years. I wouldn't want to upset them. (9 years)
>
> I am frightened to tell anyone. I am so glad you asked me, I wouldn't have told you otherwise. (11 years)
>
> I tell no-one, not even the girls. I keep it to myself. They'd think I was soft. (11 years)
>
> It's too personal. I hide many things – especially the things most important to me. (13 years)
>
> No-one has ever spoken to me about it. (17 years)
>
> I don't think other people want to hear all that. You've got to hide that from the rest of the world. (19 years)
>
> I still feel like a foreigner, though I have been here for 50 years. So I couldn't confide in anyone. (8 years)
>
> It's not to be mentioned. (20 years)
>
> It is like this: people don't really believe you. (10 years)
>
> It is a thing between you and her, nothing to do with outsiders. (22 years)

Perhaps they would laugh at me, saying I am dreaming, but I don't think I am. (33 years)

I am so glad others see the same. (13 years)

I have told you more than anyone else in all these years. (14 years)

## Few people find the experience unpleasant

The majority of percipients (68.6%) are helped by the experience and find it pleasant; few (6%) find it disturbing.

I felt him touch me. It frightened me. Made you think you were going up the wall. (8 years)

When I heard his voice, I would think, 'Why he's alive,' and then I would think, 'No it can't be, he is dead.' It upset me very much, it wasn't right. (5 years)

He called, 'Mam, Mam,' from the bottom of the stairs. It frightened me. I didn't answer because they say you shouldn't answer the dead. (6 years)

It wasn't right, it upset me very much. (5 years)

I find it frightening. (8 years – his young wife had committed suicide.)

## Comments by people who had no perception of the dead

I'd never wish him back to suffer what he did go through. (6 years)

I had the children and the farm on my hands. (6 years)

He was very difficult to do with. (9 years)

He was cruel to me. (14 years)

I have often wished I could see him, if only for a minute, but I've never seen him. (16 years)

I wish I could have, I would have liked his advice. (48 years)

Saw enough of him when he was alive. We were not suited like my second husband. (64 years)

## A dilemma for the Clergy

The attitude of the Church to experiences like those discussed here is ambiguous. It is probably less dismissive now than formerly, and priests and pastors are becoming more aware, and empathetic, to such disclosures, but many clergy still have difficulty in discussing them openly and in placing them within a theological context. Usually these experiences do not come soon after death; they are not part of the immediate grief process and are more likely to occur many weeks or months later. So they are not part of the expected agenda for pre-burial counselling or for the eulogy given during the funeral service.

I have never heard these occurrences mentioned in a sermon, though when one considers the age and widowed state of many congregations this seems like a good opportunity often missed. However, I do remember bereavement being discussed at length in a sermon preached on an Easter Sunday by a bishop, and that it was beautifully delivered and carefully prepared. The bishop spoke movingly about the way bereavement can affect people's lives, mentioning in particular the anger and despair that often accompany grief. The bishop spoke at length about Jesus' meeting with the women – how very glad they were to see him and how he had sent them to tell the disciples of his reappearance, making them 'apostles to the Apostles' and thus ensuring that the first account of the Resurrection was given to men by women. But I knew that one element would be missing and that nothing would be said of people's perceptions of their own beloved dead in the world today. This omission is difficult to understand because it merely avoids discussing events that have a special affinity with the Resurrection. It is a taboo subject, possibly for two reasons. The first is that the frequency, normality and helpfulness of these events was not established until quite recently. Second, there seems to have been a long tradition within the Church not to discuss the theological significance of these aspects of bereavement. One wonders why. Perhaps some are too close in kind to the Resurrection appearances of Jesus himself and the early Church needed to maintain a distance between these different, though in some ways similar, events. There is also the prohibition against any contact with the dead, long embedded in Judaism and subsequently part of the Christian tradition. This is an enormously powerful form of censure and is perhaps one of the reasons, together with the deeply personal nature of such experiences, why the bereaved have been reluctant to talk of these experiences in the past.

The bereaved speak more openly now about their perceived encounters with the dead than formerly, but it remains a topic that many hesitate to mention to the clergy. In most churches, ministers are likely to regard these experiences in a sympathetic and non-denunciatory manner, but sometimes pastors do ascribe a demonic origin to them, saying that they require treatment by deliverance or even exorcism. Attitudes can vary greatly between and within denominations. Within the Anglican Church, the opinion expressed by the Christian Deliverance Study Group in its book *Deliverance: Psychic Deliverance and Occult Involvement* is sensible and helpful. It includes the following statement: 'Exorcism may be positively harmful if it is not the right treatment. It should be used for those cases where non-human malevolent influence is suspected. Human spirits whether incarnate, earthbound, or discarnate should not be exorcized. They do not need banishment to hell but loving care and pastoral concern. When a person is disturbed by the attention of discarnate humans, prayer, blessing and the requiem Eucharist are more appropriate than attempts at banishment.' [10] This statement is very much line with the teaching of Dr McAll on the role of the Eucharist in dealing with ancestral problems, though whether the Study Group agrees with his belief that such problems can cause illness is not clear.

I do not know if the perceptions of the bereaved are due to discarnate human spirits, but I do know that few people are troubled by them and in my experience none are sufficiently disturbed to seek medical help. Regarding the use of deliverance and exorcism in bereavement, it is worth remembering that exorcism is not a specifically Christian practise and that it is widely used by priests of other traditions. The time has probably come for Christians to move away from such practices and to cease portraying as abnormal that which is good and healthy.

## Letters from the widowed

The following are letters from people who wrote to me after reading a letter about widowhood that was published in the *Church Times* in March 2000. They speak of the bereaved's need for the Church to take their experiences seriously.

*From Mr CB*

I was interested and greatly encouraged by your letter in the *Church Times* re. 'presence of the deceased'. Shortly before Christmas, I lost my beloved wife. I had known her for some 56 years and we were very close. Some little while ago, I had gone up to our bedroom, preparing to lie down when she was there, so real I could reach out to her. She said, 'I love you dear.' In a few moments she had gone but I felt wonderful. It happened just as you said, spontaneously and unexpectedly. I had not been thinking of anything in particular. It was not simply a dream. I was holding my little cat who was with me at the time.

I spoke of this, in confidence, to one of our clergy who received it sympathetically but I felt that I was being regarded as a potential candidate for the 'funny farm'; I am after all 75 years old, and at that age, well! The event spoken of was not at night but late on a sunny afternoon. More recently I was in the dining room, She was there, I put my arms around her, she was as real and warm as I knew her. She smiled and was gone. I have not mentioned this later experience to anyone. Again it was in the daytime. I have never before experienced any paranormal event.

I am a Reader, now in my 20th year, and have conducted some hundreds of funerals. When my wife died there was this awful feeling; was there really life after death? I have just finished a sermon based on John 20:19–31, it seems to me that Christ appearing among the disciples, even though the doors were locked against intruders, is not such a fanciful thought at all. There is still this awful gap in my life and the grief still hurts, but somehow there is something else too.

*From a church organist*

I have just read your letter in the *Church Times* and having lost a dear husband a few years ago, your observations were very interesting. For a long time now and before my husband's death I have been concerned about the attitude of the clergy to death and the question of the afterlife. We are taught about the Resurrection of Christ in detail, but when it comes to serious discussion, and asking how that teaching affects, as you say, the common experiences of humanity, the questions are 'skirted around' and in doing so are no comfort to those who grieve the loss of a loved one.

My friend's husband who is a sacristan in my church had the wonderful experience of having my husband, who died two months earlier, sit by him all during a funeral service. I was nearby – as I was playing the organ for the service. He described my husband who had been churchwarden for many years, in detail. My friend's husband is not a 'fanciful' man, he is very 'down to earth' and it was a tremendous emotional experience for him. He is a man of 78 years and has never had any kind of spiritual experience before. He was very moved by this and, after being reassured by his wife that I would not be upset, he told me what had happened. I was overwhelmed and so happy to know that my husband is still with me.

It is a shame that this, and countless other experiences that you speak of are not taken seriously by the clergy in general. Christ's Resurrection is preached but it seems that to bring it down to our level is ignored. We are indeed separated; and our transformation beyond this life, confirmed by so many encounters, by so many people, is never mentioned. I trust that your wish that this subject will be considered and discussed in theological colleges will come about and be acted upon.

*From Mrs SF*

I am writing to thank you for your recent letter in the *Church Times* and tell you of my experiences. My husband died in 1980. About three months after his death as I was waking after a restless night, worrying about something that had to be done the following day, I had a very strong feeling of his presence and felt his hands on my shoulders. This was not a dream – it was a very real experience.

My mother died five years ago and some time after her death I was aware of her presence, but this time did not feel the physical touch. I have never related these experiences before, not even to the family. Partially because I thought they would not be understood, but mainly because they were extremely personal, spiritual and precious moments, which were mine and I did not need or want to share them. Until I read your letter I was not aware how common an experience this is. Maybe others like me do not want to talk about them – but perhaps we should, especially in the context of Resurrection.

You are probably right when you say that the theology of the Resurrection has generally become too intellectualised, but we are very fortunate here in having a parish priest who very much places it in the present and within common experience.

*From Mr L (a 70-year-old widower)*

As a result of your letter in the *Church Times* I wish to inform you of the personal relief and reassurance I received from it. If it had not been printed I doubt if I could have spoken to anyone about the experience I had a few weeks ago. The experience happened during the night. I had retired to bed at approximately 10 pm. I had not taken any stimulants whatsoever, unable to sleep I lay in bed thinking of what I would do the following day. I heard the Grandmother clock in the hall strike 11 pm and shortly afterwards I sensed someone in bed beside me. I knew immediately it was my wife. She put her arm about me as she did in life, I sensed a tender warm feeling that was so natural. I then turned to face her but her face was just a blur. I then spoke to her and said, 'You shouldn't be here you know,' and she replied, 'I know,' and then she left me with a feeling of intense pleasure and comfort. I then heard the clock strike quarter past 11. The whole experience I judge to have taken between 2-3 minutes and I was wide awake the whole time.

As a result of your letter, I was able to approach my local Rector and told him of what had occurred, he was very understanding and sympathetic. He told me that many people had related similar experiences to him during his ministry which I found very reassuring as I was beginning to wonder if I was a one-off freak. Only last night I showed your letter to two ladies who had been bereaved. I know one of them had a similar experience in broad daylight. I was in her company on holiday with 22 other people. We were crossing a very busy street in Paphos, Cyprus, on getting to the other side of the road she burst into tears, I went to comfort her and she told me her husband had taken her hand and helped her across the road. The other lady told me that she was constantly in contact with her husband asking for help and instructions and receiving them. May I conclude with the following information – the 2 ladies and myself are fully committed and practising Christians. We have a great faith that has sustained us through our sad times but we have sure and certain knowledge that we will meet our loved ones once again in the Good Lord's own, and not our, time. This has not been an easy letter to write please excuse its length.

## The range of experiences

Most aspects of human life can be placed within a normal distribution curve. This is a mathematical device that enables the normality of a person's behaviour and attributes – e.g. height and intelligence – to be compared with those of other people. Thus we talk of people being of normal height and of being short or tall; similarly we know that the light that we can perceive is part of a broad spectrum that includes the colours red to violet, but extends beyond this narrow band into those ranges that include the infra-red and ultra-violet frequencies. We know intellectually of the existence of infra-red and UV light but we cannot appreciate them with our eyes in the way that most people can see the different colours.

We know that while many people can hear perfectly adequately, some are tone-deaf and others are completely deaf. Similarly some people are colour-blind whilst others may be completely blind or just partially sighted. We accept these things as part of the infinite variety of human life. We should extend this acceptance to our understanding of the subjective experiences of the bereaved. The most important finding of the survey is that a perception of a dead spouse is both a common and a normal consequence of bereavement. On the other hand, not having these experiences is an equally common and normal finding among widowed people.

How then should we respond to people who say that they are aware of the presence of their dead loved one? Firstly with interest; we should not classify them as being in any way mentally ill or odd. Psychiatrists accept the normality of these bereavement perceptions but some GPs continue to diagnose them wrongly. Dr John Roberts, a former Professor of Psychological Medicine in New Zealand, pointed this out in an article in which he reported seeing a Maori woman in the last out-patient clinic of his career in an English hospital. She had married an English soldier during World War II and had settled in the UK afterwards. She had never returned to New Zealand and felt quite isolated in the Wirral when her husband died. She had been referred for a psychiatric assessment by her GP who thought she was 'crazy' as she believed that her husband and the spirits of the tribal elders were visiting her. Such experiences are regarded as normal by the Maoris and during the consultation Dr Roberts was able to reassure the woman that he knew this and accepted it. He wrote:

> 'Relief spread across her face as she found she could talk about such matters without being regarded as odd. This gave me considerable pleasure, but more importantly I hope that it gave her some lasting comfort. That I had some understanding of her culture was an aid in helping her. In fact, I now think that had I not known about her culture I too might have believed she was psychotically ill.' [11]

It is an interesting possibility that this lady could easily have been given psychotropic drugs by another doctor, been treated with 'deliverance' by a Christian minister, or exorcised by a pagan priest. All she needed was understanding and reassurance.

## 'Hallucinations'

The inappropriateness of the words used when discussing these experiences of the bereaved is a constant problem. One retired priest put it this way: 'When I first heard a hospital chaplain speak of the 'hallucinations' of the bereaved I was quite shocked, and he seemed thereby to dismiss them as wishful thinking. Only later did I realize that medics use the term in a specialized sense, much as theologians do with 'myths'. For to the layman, the one means 'something that is not there', the other 'something that is not true'.'

Much of the initial work in this field was done by psychiatrists, so the term 'hallucination' tended to be used when the first research papers were published. Doubts about the appropriateness of the term arose only when these experiences of the bereaved were shown to be common, normal and helpful. There is now general agreement among psychiatrists that the term 'hallucination' is not appropriate for an experience that has none of the features of a psychotic illness or that can be linked with any of the other causes of hallucinations. Such causes include the use of psychedelic drugs, alcoholism, acute toxic states and the withdrawal of drugs from people who have become dependent upon them. The word 'hallucination' fails to convey the normality of the experiences and points instead to the possibility that bereaved people who report them may be mentally deranged, which is not the case. These experiences are sometimes called 'pseudo-hallucinations' but this is also inappropriate. A new, generally acceptable, terminology is needed.

One further point needs to be made. This was also stated by Dr John Roberts who wrote to me as follows: 'From the psychiatric point of view, the experiences which your subjects describe are different from those described by our patients when they are disturbed. The hallucinations when the brain is intact and not subject to exogenous substances are almost exclusively auditory. I have never been told about visual hallucinations by patients who were psychotic in a schizophrenic way unless they had taken a drug of some sort. If the brain is damaged or under the influence of a 'mind altering' substance, then visual hallucinations are common to the almost total exclusion of auditory hallucinations. The experiences of your subjects are quite unlike those of our patients.' [12]

## Significant dreams

In planning this study of widowhood, I decided not to include dreams and only to accept accounts of events that occurred whilst the individual was wide awake and fully conscious. This was a correct decision to make at the time and was endorsed by the senior psychiatrists who oversaw the project. However, some people say that relevant dreams can be of immense significance and should have been included. I understand their concern and offer, as an example, extracts from a letter that I received from a lady who I met, after speaking at a conference in 2003:

> 'Thank you so much for your interest in our discussions and inviting me to write down some of my experiences although the written

word will fall short of conveying the depths of these experiences. Five months before the end of war in '44 my dearly loved fiancé, a flying officer pilot on Lancaster bombers, was killed when his plane developed engine trouble over the South Downs. Reports confirmed that he made heroic efforts to keep the plane (laden with bombs and incendiaries) airborne over the town of Worthing and tragically it crashed in shallow water when the tide was out. Damage was done to some properties on the front but the town was saved. All on board were killed. The crash occurred 10 days before our wedding date and my life changed completely.

About 6 months later, during sleep, having earnestly prayed that I may not wake in the morning, I became aware that Fred was coming. Dressed in full uniform and, kneeling beside my bed, he spoke in a quiet, grave manner which was infinitely reassuring. Upon leaving I asked if he would come again, to which he quietly said he would come whenever I needed him most. In the morning I found the bedroom filled with sunlight – as it was on his visit – and the miracle was the joyous transformation his visit had produced, bringing light into darkness and depression.'

She mentions other encounters with her fiancé and also with her parents. Of the former she says, 'His presence is often with me.' The letter concludes with these words:

'Having thankfully been brought up with a religious background, I am immensely grateful for my deeper experiences of the continuity of life after the death of the physical body which relates so wonderfully with the teachings of Christ.'

Having read the letter, one thing continues to puzzle me. It is a technical point but perhaps worth mentioning. In her letter and in a note that my correspondent wrote later, she made a distinction between dreams and the sleep state in which she says her experiences of Fred occurred. She wrote: 'All my contacts with Fred have been in the sleep state, these experiences are more real and significant than dreams, which can sometimes leave us sad upon awakening, but meeting him in the sleep state left me upon wakening with the strong conviction of joy and anticipation of the continuity of life as we read in the Gospels. The contacts have been so real and positive.'

Her final comment reminds me of the visions seen by Peter at Joppa and by Paul in the temple at Jerusalem, when they received the most significant of spiritual insights whilst in a trance. If questioned now, I wonder how they would describe their state of mind when the visions appeared – would they say it was a sleep state, a dream or speak of it in some other way? Another question arises. Now that medical science is advancing rapidly in its understanding of the structure and physiology of the nervous system, will future scientists be able to provide us with a greater insight into the nature of these revelations than was available 2,000 years ago or even now?

## Comment/Summary

Belief in an afterlife is a tenet that has been held consistently by all races for many ages. There are, and always have been, dissenting voices but the strength of this belief is remarkable and its persistence merits investigation. Without some constant input into the universal psyche, such a belief is likely to fade away and this chapter considers one factor that is pertinent to such views being maintained. It deals with the experiences of the bereaved, in particular the extent to which widowed people believe that they have direct contact with their deceased spouses. It gives data on the incidence of such occurrences, the different types of perceptions that are reported, their independence of social criteria such as age, gender, residence and religious practices, and most importantly on their helpfulness and normality. The findings have been replicated by studies in Iceland, the UK and the US, but continue to be omitted from the Church's teaching on the Resurrection and afterlife. This is surprising, as they enhance the evidence for the Resurrection rather than diminishing its importance.

One difference between the Easter appearances and those reported by the widowed is worth noting here. Widowed people's experiences of their dead spouses tend to occur weeks or months after the person's death; in contrast, Jesus appeared to his friends soon after the Crucifixion. Another phenomenon peculiar to the Resurrection is reported in Matthew's Gospel (27: 53). There we are told that that 'many holy people who had come out of their tombs when Jesus died, entered Jerusalem after his Resurrection and were seen by many people'. I have never heard this discussed in church but surely it merits some comment, not just silent evasion. Finally, the following assessment by a widow may usefully conclude the chapter. She said, 'We all have our doubts about whether there is a life after death, but when you have experiences like this you feel elated afterwards and know it is true'.

CHAPTER 11

# Are the Experiences Comparable?

THIS CHAPTER CONSIDERS THE experiences of the bereaved
in a more analytical and controversial way. Specifically, it
advances the case for the Christian Church to include within
its theology of the Resurrection, people's experiences of their
dead loved ones. Chapter 10 has indicated the basis on which
this suggestion is advocated. Here the reasons for doing so
are discussed in greater detail. The opposing views of Gerald
O'Collins SJ have been mentioned briefly in earlier chapters; here
they are examined more closely and for that reason readers may
find the following biographical note helpful. Born in Australia,
Gerald O'Collins is a Jesuit priest and a distinguished Catholic
theologian. He is a former Professor of Systematic Theology
at the Gregorian University in Rome and was also Dean of its
theology faculty. He is now Research Professor in Theology at St
Mary's University College in Twickenham, England.

In his response to my questionnaire, one Anglican bishop
included the following pertinent remark: 'The question you will
have to face will be: Is there any difference between the post-
Resurrection appearances of Christ (i.e. before the Ascension)
and the occurrences to individuals today?' My answer to the
question is yes, there are major differences, but it is also important
to consider the possibility that the divide is not absolute and to
seek, where possible, appropriate similarities. In his comparison

of the Easter appearances with the experiences of the widowed, Gerald O'Collins says that 'detailed comparison shows up serious differences' and that any analogy is 'not close or illuminating'. [1] This last assessment is valid in part, but it gives no credence to the finding that bereavement brings a range of experiences including some that do resemble the Easter appearances. The particular objections raised by Professor O'Collins are considered in detail at the end of this chapter.

First let us consider the question of analogies. To be analogous means to be similar yet different. Two objects or situations may resemble each other without being identical and their differences, whatever they may be – perhaps in size or function – are obvious, but despite the disparities certain points of similarity cannot be denied. It is from this perspective that the experiences of bereaved people, and of those who claim to have encountered Jesus in recent years, should be considered alongside the accounts recorded in the Gospels. This does not diminish the significance of the Resurrection but it does allow people to acknowledge the reality of their own experiences and relate them to what many regard as the most important event in the history of the human race.

Examples of what I understand by analogies may be useful here. Three instances are offered. The first applies to mountainous regions. The highest mountain in the world is Everest, while Mount Snowdon is the highest in Wales. Both are mountains but they are not identical. The difference in size is obvious and they possess many other features that differentiate them. Their terrain is totally different, they provide habitats for different forms of life and they were created in different ways. The mountain region of North Wales was formed from an ancient continent that became denuded through aeons of time, and was later transformed by volcanic heat and pressure. Everest stands in a mountain range which appeared when the continental plates of Asia and India collided within the depths of the oceans and pushed up part of the existing Asian continent to create the Himalayas. They are similar but different.

The second analogy deals with sacrifice. Christians accept that in his Passion and Crucifixion, Jesus made a full, perfect and complete sacrifice for the sins of the whole world. Nothing can be added to or retracted from it, but in our daily lives we are meant to follow his example and offer our own sacrifices as he did. In this we seek to align ourselves with him whilst accepting the intrinsic differences.

The third example is more clearly biblical. It deals with our relationship with Jesus and with the Father. At the beginning of the fourth Gospel, the evangelist describes Jesus as 'the only begotten Son'. At the end of the same book the risen Christ tells Mary Magdalene to 'Go to my brothers, and tell them that I am returning to my Father and to your Father, to my God and your God' (John 20: 17). Previously Jesus had spoken of 'the Father' or of 'my Father'. Now in Resurrection he adds 'your Father', confirming that like him, we are children of God. This does not place us in the same relationship with the Father as Jesus, but it draws us close to him so that we are incorporated into his Sonship by the grace of adoption.

## The present need

Gerald O'Collins says that detailed comparisons cannot be made between the experiences of the bereaved and those of the disciples who met Jesus after the Resurrection. I accept that major differences exist in the significance of the events and the spiritual stature of those involved, but I believe comparisons can be made and in fact should be made. A theology of the Resurrection is incomplete if the observations of the bereaved are not incorporated into it. One cannot say that Jesus died and lives, and that this was proved by his Resurrection 2,000 years ago, and that people's experiences of their dead relatives today must bear no relationship to that fact. The experiences of the bereaved are sometimes explained away in psychological terms, and this I have shown in *Death and Bereavement* without considering the reasons appropriate. [2] However, if these experiences can be explained away, then the same arguments must be applied to the disciples' encounters with the risen Jesus. If this is not done, then it must be clearly shown why one phenomenon is illusory and the other a reality, and the explanations be given in terms that most people will understand. That Christians who maintain their contact with the Church consider this to be necessary is apparent from the letters quoted in the previous chapter. It is not the laity alone who seek clarification, it is a dilemma that also troubles ordained ministers, as the following letter from an Anglican priest indicates:

> Thank you for your letter to the *Church Times* regarding reported contacts from dead loved ones. This is the first time I have read or heard anything on the subject. I have been ordained nearly five years in parish ministry and I have visited and spoken with probably 100–150 people about their deceased relatives. I have heard a very large number of consistent accounts of contact as described in your letter. I find it hard to dismiss these reports as simple emotionalism or folk religion, but I struggle to find any way of accepting the reports as true or having a context against the teaching of the Bible.
>
> I trained at... College and my beliefs are consistent with evangelical theology. My initial response to these reports was that these people were expressing a wish based on the folk religion or pursuing relief through practices which might be similar to those used by mediums and the like. An alternative explanation might be that it was the Lord revealing his Love to them in some way which they mistook for comfort from the dead loved one. I am uncomfortable with both these theories.
>
> Today I am to conduct the funeral of a 15-month-old child. The young mother's only expressed wish was that she might hear from

her son, that he would tell her that he was now well and did not blame her for his death. I was unable to offer her such a hope. I can only pray that Jesus might speak into her life and release her from some of the pain.

If there is a 'healthy' theology to support after-death contact I might at least allow a hope that her wish was met or even intercede on her behalf. Perhaps you can suggest some reading on the subject which will allow me to reintegrate and reaffirm the value of such experiences under our understanding of the Resurrection of Christ.

Yours sincerely.

The anguish in this letter is obvious; so too is the minister's concern for the mother and her need for reassurance. Many of the reports provided by the bereaved give the type of reassurance that the mother wants, and some have been recounted in this book. But in the final analysis, mothers (and of course other family members) need their own personal assurance that their child's life on earth has been fulfilled and that in some inexplicable way the life continues elsewhere. As a Christian doctor I can only share the information I possess and my personal certainty that life continues beyond death. Death is a bridge which separates us from our loved ones but, as many widowed people can testify, the separation is not complete though the anguish of loss can be great. In the parable of Dives and Lazarus the gulf cannot be crossed over, but God in his wisdom uses many methods to reassure his perplexed children that 'Christ is risen' and that our loved ones are risen with him. It is for theologians to express this certainty in terms that are acceptable to the Church and people in general.

Keith Ward (Regius Professor of Divinity, University of Oxford) has indicated how this may be done from the perspective of modern physics. Quoting the works of Dyson, Tipler and Smolin, he says, 'The idea of a life after death, in some other sort of universe, when these physical bodies have decayed, comes to seem much more plausible in the light of these far-future speculations of physics.' Speaking specifically of Jesus' Resurrection, he says, 'It becomes plausible to think that his body always was, like all physical bodies, an appearance to human minds of a deeper unimaginable reality. It could be instantaneously transformed into another form (a spiritual body) in another space time... The unique thing about Jesus' transformation would be that his transfigured body appeared in solid physical form, for short and intermittent periods, for some time after his death.' [3]

## What help is there for grieving parents?

What help can the parochial clergy offer the young mother mentioned above? They will of course be knowledgeable about the stages of bereavement, of the psychological and social support that is available, and of the Church's teaching on the Resurrection and the afterlife, but this is not going to allay her grief. Above all, this mother wants her child back, preferably to hold and nurture, but as this is not possible she wants to be convinced that the child is alive and well. At present this reassurance is something that Christian doctrine does not provide. Yet for many bereaved people the conviction that their loved ones have survived death comes naturally and quite unexpectedly. Not everyone is blessed in this way and it may take time to become apparent, as CS Lewis discovered. He found that months had to elapse following the death of his wife before he could write in his notebook:

> 'Suddenly something quite unexpected has happened... when I mourned H. least, I remembered her best. Indeed it was something better than memory; an instantaneous unanswerable impression. To say it was like meeting would be going too far. Yet there was that in it which tempts one to use those words... I said several notebooks ago, that if I got what seemed like an assurance of H's presence, I wouldn't believe it. Easier said than done... It was quite incredibly unemotional. Just the impression of her mind facing my own... Much like getting a telephone call or wire from her

about some practical arrangement... Yet there was an extreme and cheerful intimacy... The intimacy was complete, sharply bracing and restorative too'. [4]

Such encounters do happen; they cannot be guaranteed but they do reinforce people's belief in a life after death and should be recognized by the Church as such. They provide a means of sustaining hope and easing the anguish of the bereft.

I am reminded of a young man who was severely disabled after breaking his neck in a diving accident. He had limited movements in his arms but eventually regained the ability to drive a car, hold down a job and enjoy the company of his friends. For months after the accident he was suicidal. His wife left him and when he returned home from hospital he was completely dependent on his mother – a frail, elderly lady who had to wash, lift, feed and toilet him. Then his sister was murdered, both disasters befalling the family before I knew them. Visiting that house was always an uplifting occasion and I invariably felt better for having done so. Knowing of their Christian faith, I asked the mother how she had managed to cope with so much grief and such heavy nursing responsibilities and remain cheerful and active within the village community. She told me that it was because she had had a vision in which she had seen her daughter looking beautiful and radiant and she knew that she was alright. The experience had sustained her and reinforced her Christian belief, but not every bereaved parent is so blessed. It is interesting that she spoke of the appearance as a visionary one; for her it was supernatural.

In contrast, most widowed people speak in a down-to-earth way about their meetings with their dead partners. They know that the person is present with them – they can often see them and sometimes touch them and feel the warmth of their bodies. This closeness can be so intimate that when Mr C wrote of meeting his wife in the dining room, he said: 'She was there, I put my arms around her, she was as real and warm as I knew her.' There is something familiar about this statement; it brings to mind the Gospel account of the women meeting Jesus at the Resurrection and clasping his feet. The reality of both experiences is stated explicitly, and such reports are important in helping us to understand better the significance of the Resurrection and that life does continue after death.

## Sharing experiences

The Compassionate Friends is a voluntary organization that was established to enable bereaved parents to share their anguish with similarly afflicted people. Its founders found that it was by sharing experiences in this way that their grief was most effectively eased. So I offer a story that may help distressed clergy and parents. It was told to me by a friend whose son had committed suicide in the prime of life, and differs from other accounts given here in that her experience occurred at night after she had gone to sleep.

My friend's son, Simon, was a paranoid schizophrenic. He was well known to me, having been a patient of mine in his late teens and early twenties, though he was not a patient when he killed himself. He could be charming, manipulative and often violent. The day before he died, mother and son walked together in the fields and she remembered it as being a lovely time together. Simon had often expressed suicidal thoughts and she remembered him saying, 'Of course, Mum, you know I wouldn't kill myself.' The next day, in the presence of a psychiatric nurse, he jumped through the window of a high-story flat to his death in the street below. The body was battered so badly that his mother was not allowed to see the corpse, but she knew from the chalk markings in the street that his right arm had been severed from the rest of his body. Her grief was so intense it could not be evaluated. Then, a few weeks later whilst asleep at night she awoke to see Simon sitting on the bed. He looked well and happy and she heard him say, 'Oh, Mum.' She stretched out her arms to embrace him and as she did so he disappeared. She knew it was not a dream because, although she had not felt his weight pressing down, the imprint of his body where he had sat on the bed was clearly visible. Following this experience, the mother found that although she continued to grieve for Simon, sometimes very deeply, she was able to cope much better than formerly. It was an experience she shared with her daughter who was also grieving deeply.

Although she spoke of Simon's appearance to her daughter, she told no-one about the vision of Jesus she had had much earlier. I was the first to learn of it, and it happened in this way. We had gone to a church in Oxford which was celebrating its patronal feast, St Mary Magdalene. During the return journey, Simon's death was mentioned and discussed. I asked her if she had any other experiences. She hesitated and then said that yes, she had seen Jesus. This happened some thirty years previously, at a time when she was very angry with the Church because of the way her vicar had treated a friend. She was so angry that she stopped going to church even though she was a long-standing member of the choir and was involved in other ways. One night, she was asleep and awoke to see the face of Jesus looking at her through the window. Nothing was said and the vision was short-lived but she was sure it was Jesus. Two consequences followed this vision. She resumed church attendance; and the face she saw at the window remains imprinted in her mind. It is a gentle, caring, olive-skinned face with brown eyes, longish hair and a short beard.

## Hallucinations and visions

Sceptics find it hard to accept that the perceptions of the bereaved can have any spiritual significance; they prefer to deny the reality of the experiences and tend to dismiss them as hallucinations or visions. This was probably as true in biblical times as it is today. That the term 'hallucination' is a misnomer has been discussed already; similarly the word 'vision' does not describe the perceptions correctly as there is usually no visual component in the experiences of the bereaved. Almost half of all widowed people have occasions when they are aware of the presence of the dead spouse but only 12 per cent see their beloved ones. These are not visions in the sense of being supernatural apparitions – the bereaved do not encounter angelic or heavenly personages, only individuals they know well and in environments that are normal and familiar – *viz.* their own kitchens, gardens or dining rooms. They rarely speak of them as visions.

In his book *The Resurrection of the Son of God*, NT Wright points out that we are not dealing with a new phenomenon and that people have known for a very long time that such meetings with the dead do occur. This is true: Shakespeare drew on this tradition in *Hamlet* and also for his depiction of Queen Katherine's deathbed scene in *Henry VIII*. But the frequency, helpfulness and normality of such meetings has not been part of common knowledge, and there is still a tendency in the Western world to diminish their significance and deny them an appropriate place within the belief system of Christianity. This point may be illustrated by considering the contents of two recent and important books on the Resurrection. The multi-author book *Resurrection, Theological and Scientific Assessments* [5] says nothing about the experiences of the bereaved and NT Wright's major work of over 800 pages refers to them very briefly. As noted above, Bishop Wright does say that 'such seeing, even such meetings occur and that people have known about them throughout recorded history' but he makes no attempt to set out their relevance for pastoral care today. [6] This indifference caused John Roberts, a retired Professor of Psychiatry, to point out that recent writings on the subject by psychiatrists 'have been almost entirely ignored by theologians'. [7] Such indifference is no longer acceptable. Theologians need to consider more carefully, and positively, the new insights provided by psychiatric studies.

There is no denying that the bereaved have been very reluctant to talk about their perceptions of the dead, which may help to explain why, in the past, our knowledge of these events was so scanty and distorted. During my interviews with the widowed, I found that surprisingly few people felt able to tell others of their experiences and that they kept them secret from even close friends and relatives. This was even the normal practice following a remarriage. On the occasions when I discussed the subject with widows who had remarried and the second husband was present during the conversation, it was often obvious that he was learning for the first time that his wife had instances when she felt that her dead spouse was very close to her. Similarly, when speaking on the subject at a meeting of Welsh psychiatrists in the 1970s, a senior doctor challenged my figures, citing as his reason that he had never encountered any such cases during his long career (over 30 years) as a psychiatrist. Most doctors may have shared his reservations at the time, as the subject was not mentioned in any text books of medicine or psychiatry. Luckily this dearth of information has been addressed and the frequency and helpfulness of the experiences is now widely accepted by health care workers.

The question that must be asked now is: why did people decide to keep such significant experiences a secret? I have quoted in the preceding chapter some of the reasons the widowed gave, but no one mentioned another possibly important reason: fear. In the past, medical practitioners were respected but also feared in a way that no longer applies. At critical moments in people's lives their decisions could be decisive, not just in matters of life and death. Most had the power to certify as insane, and commit to an asylum, anyone who was regarded as mentally disturbed, and speaking of meeting the dead could easily fall into that category. The clergy could not be trusted either. They could be expected to denounce such talk as sinful and contrary to Christian belief, and would warn their flock against dabbling with spiritualism and the occult. They might even raise the possibility of demonic possession and propose a service to expel the demon. This rite is not an anachronism; it is still widely performed and its use seems to be on the increase in some churches. The terminology has been changed – exorcism is now commonly referred to as 'deliverance' – but it is a form of ministry that is practised within mainstream Christian communities and the reasons for doing so can include possession by the spirits of the dead. It is useful to remember that exorcism is not a specifically Christian rite. It is practised in many countries and its practitioners include probably more animists, Buddhists, Hindus and Muslims than Christians. [8]

In the Middle Ages demonic possession was often associated with accusations of witchcraft, and folk-memory does not readily forget the witch hunts that became part of the European landscape after the Reformation. This affected mainly the Protestant countries of Northern Europe and the victims were predominantly women. In the UK, Scottish law dealt very severely with suspected witches, but English law was different in that many women were accused of witchcraft but few were tortured to extract confessions. The penalties imposed in England and its colonies tended to be lighter than those in other North European countries, but the revised Witchcraft Act of 1563 did impose the death penalty on those found guilty of consulting a witch or medium, and a new Act in 1642 was even more severe. All these Acts against sorcery were repealed by the British Parliament in 1735, but the Witchcraft Act of the same year still made it illegal to act as a spiritualist medium and to practise telepathy or clairvoyance. This Act was repealed only in 1951 when it was replaced by the Fraudulent

Medium Act which legalized those activities provided they were not performed for monetary gain. The Western world has a long history of repressing any suggested contact with the dead, which can be traced back to biblical times when Saul, King of Israel (c. 1030 BCE) expelled all mediums from his kingdom. Having said that, it is necessary to emphasize that the phenomena being discussed here occur quite spontaneously in clear consciousness, and are not associated in any way with the participation of mediums.

## The denial of any analogy

In his book *Easter Faith,* Gerald O'Collins gives five reasons for rejecting the possibility of an analogy existing between the post-Resurrection experiences of the disciples and those reported by the bereaved. His assessment, which differs from mine, merits careful consideration and a detailed response. My reply to his objections is given schematically.

1) Objection

Jesus made extraordinary claims about his mission and identity and there is no such element in the accounts given by the bereaved.

Response

This is a valid comment but it is not relevant to the point under discussion. Jesus' extraordinary nature and the relevance of his life, Crucifixion and Resurrection is not in dispute, but these attributes do not rule out the possibility of the widowed finding in their own experiences evidence for Christ's promise of eternal life which complements that provided in the Gospel stories.

## 2) Objection

The Gospel stories tell of Jesus appearing to groups of people whilst the experiences reported by bereaved relatives are encounters with the beloved on a very personal basis.

## Response

Certainly there were occasions when Jesus appeared to more than one person at the Resurrection but the experiences of the bereaved can also occur within a social context. Two of the letters quoted in the previous chapter state this clearly. In one instance the beloved took hold of the widow's hand as she accompanied her friends across the road in Cyprus. Another tells how her dead husband sat alongside the verger during a church service whilst she, the widow, played the organ nearby. In both instances, other people were present even though they were unaware of what had happened. A greater group awareness does distinguish the Gospel stories from those recounted by the currently bereaved. Why this should be so, we do not know but it might have been due to the close bonding of the disciples and to the dramatic, and perhaps dangerous, circumstances that surrounded the Crucifixion and Resurrection.

Two other points are of interest. Firstly, little importance tends to be given to the Resurrection of the dead that accompanied Christ's death. Yet we are told that the tombs 'were opened and many bodies of the saints who had fallen asleep were raised…and went into the holy city and appeared to many' (Matthew 27: 51–53). Similarly, surprisingly little information is provided about Christ's appearance to the five hundred, or of his Ascension, even though it was witnessed by the eleven; nor is it made clear why some of them doubted even at this late stage that he was truly risen (Matthew 28: 17; Mark 16: 14).

3) Objection

There was a dramatic change in the lifestyle of the disciples following the Resurrection and no comparable change is apparent in the lives of those who encounter their beloved dead.

Response

According to the Gospels, the disciples were in hiding immediately after the Resurrection. They were fearful, dejected and disbelieving and did nothing to proclaim the Good News. The dramatic changes in lifestyle occurred after Pentecost and were the direct result of the descent of the Holy Spirit. Also there is little biblical evidence to support the idea that the women who met Jesus at the tomb altered their lifestyle in any significant way following the Resurrection. Their attitude to life, death and their relationship with Jesus may have changed but it seems unlikely that they would have replaced their normal household chores with other activities.

Widowhood brings its own change in lifestyle. Adjusting to this new development with its altered economic and social status can be very demanding, and whilst in some instances it may provide increased opportunities for community service, this is not the norm – especially for those living at subsistence level. For the most part we are dealing also with a different gender and age group. Jesus' closest followers were men in the prime of life who had been able to leave their normal occupations and family commitments to be with him. Now that he was ascended they were free, trained and empowered by the Holy Spirit to carry out his final command to 'go to all peoples and make them my disciples'.

Being a follower of Jesus does not require everyone to go out and set the world ablaze. The best work is often done in a quieter, less dramatic way. Mary, his mother, knew this and widowhood, like motherhood, often brings internal changes to which the individual has to adapt. These changes may include a sense of being protected, of being guided, of inner tranquillity and of no longer being afraid of darkness or loneliness. The assurance that there is more to life than its earthly span, which the bereavement experiences bring, does affect people's decisions in ways that have been mentioned in Chapter 10. The instances given included decisions not to proceed with an agreed marriage, to abstain from alcohol and to behave more circumspectly. These are not dramatic changes but they are significant and should be placed alongside the increased confidence and expansiveness displayed by Peter, James and John after Pentecost. We must remember also that the missionary zeal displayed by the eleven was variable. Our knowledge of the work undertaken by Thaddaeus, James son of Alphaeus and Simon the Cananaean is minimal, and it should not be assumed that each of these men were activists in the missionary sense of that term.

4) Objection
The bereaved tend to keep their experiences secret whilst the Apostles became missionaries and shared the Good News with others.

Response
This, of course, is true in part. People are often wary of sharing their most treasured secrets with others and some reasons for the bereaved behaving in this way have been mentioned already. However, it is evident from the letters quoted in the previous chapter that people are more willing to discuss these experiences with others than was the case forty years ago. This is due to various factors, particularly to the increased awareness that such experiences are normal and not unusual. This has come about

because of the good publicity given by the media to research work on the consequences of bereavement, the respectability given to bereavement studies by their inclusion in university courses, and through the training of counsellors by organizations such as Cruse. The differing factors that enabled the Apostles to become missionaries whilst the widowed are less likely to undertake such activities, were considered in the preceding section. Again it must be said that the Apostles did not become effective missionaries until they were empowered by the Holy Spirit at Pentecost. They seemed to have spent much of the intervening time in seclusion, maintaining a low profile, and not obviously sharing the Good News of the Resurrection with others.

## 5) Objection

The experiences of the bereaved can continue for years, whilst the Resurrection appearances of Jesus occurred over a short period of time only.

## Response

The first statement is true; the second is open to doubt for two reasons. Firstly, we do not know the time span that Jesus spent on Earth between the Resurrection and Ascension. Secondly, the argument discounts all contemporary accounts of Jesus appearing to people today even though these have been reported by a wide variety of individuals, both lay and clerical. Julian of Norwich and William Booth, the founder of the Salvation Army, are among many who were blessed with vivid perceptions of the risen Jesus.

Certainly, we know of no 'Road to Emmaus' type of meeting between Jesus and the Apostles after the Ascension, but Paul and Peter had visions of immense significance. Paul had his first encounter with the risen Jesus after the Ascension, and this took place on the road to Damascus when Paul may have been in a hypnagogic state but was probably fully alert and fully conscious. The second encounter occurred in Jerusalem when Paul says he was 'in a trance' whilst praying in the temple (Acts 22: 17-21). Both events had important consequences for Paul and the Church, but these were not isolated occasions because he speaks of other visions and of an enormous sense of being united with his risen Lord. Similarly, when Peter had a vision at Joppa, he replied to the voice that addressed him with the words: 'No, Lord, no,' (Acts 10: 14), a form of address that suggests he knew he was speaking to the risen Christ.

## Comment/summary

It is apparent from the letters quoted in Chapter 10 that widows and widowers do have experiences of their dead spouses that are similar to the Easter appearances recorded in the Gospels. This does not diminish the significance of the Resurrection but it does enable us to incorporate it into people's wider experiences of life and death. It must be remembered that only 50 per cent of widowed people have any perceived relationship with their dead spouse. Many widows and widowers, myself among them, have no such experiences but the reports of other people do confirm for me the reality of the Resurrection and the certainty that death is not the end of life but a birth into a new reality.

We must remember also that for most widowed people their experience of their deceased loved ones differs markedly from the Easter appearances of Jesus. Many have no intimation at all that their loved one is close by. Of those who do have a perception it is usually a sudden and inexplicable sense of that person's presence. For a minority the perception is clearer: perhaps a sighting and a feeling of intimacy amounting to a sense of physical closeness which, as the letters indicate, can include the warmth of bodily contact. These experiences are not objective in the sense that they can be photographed and recorded, but the absence of physical objectivity should not negate their reality. They are too common and universal to be dismissed in that way.

CHAPTER 12

# Intimations of Immortality

THIS IS A MORE discursive chapter. It brings together ideas expressed earlier and extends the discussion to include the experiences of mediaeval saints, notably St John of the Cross and Theresa of Avila. It considers the nature of Jesus' Resurrection body and how this may relate to Islam's teaching on the *Al Isra*, the Prophet Muhammad's night journey to Jerusalem and then through the seven heavens to the Sublime Throne. It begins by reviewing the experiences and opinions provided by the bishops and recorded earlier in the book.

In their responses to the questionnaire, the bishops were united in the importance they ascribed to the Resurrection, regarding it as 'central to Christian belief'. Some said that their interest in the Resurrection had grown as they grew older and were faced by personal illness and the death of loved ones. This increased awareness of their own mortality and that of others corresponds with Carl Jung's dictum that the main concern of the psyche during the second half of life is with its preparation for death. Jung considered this to be true whether the individual is consciously aware of it or not.

Although all the bishops had thought deeply about the Resurrection and were agreed about its significance, many had no fixed opinion about the nature of Jesus' Resurrection body. Only a few were sure of their position on this issue. Some were certain that Jesus had risen in a physical body but others believed that Jesus' Resurrection body was not one of flesh and blood. This differing belief among the bishops is possibly linked with the widespread acceptance of cremation in place of burial – once cremation was permitted by law late in the nineteenth century. Among the bishops who expressed a firm belief in the physical Resurrection, some said that they felt helped and supported by the testimonies of people who claim to have seen Jesus in visionary or human form. Whilst others simply expressed an acceptance of the possibility of such occurrences taking place, no bishop denied that such meetings could or do occur.

## His appearances – then and now

When Jesus appeared to his disciples at the Resurrection, he did so suddenly and unexpectedly; his departures were similarly abrupt. This pattern is reflected in reports given by people who believe they have seen Jesus recently. Not all are parallel encounters to the Easter appearances but some are, such as the occasion when Jesus walked alongside Kenneth McAll towards a Chinese village, his appearing to Fred Lemon in a locked room, and to Donald English in his wife's bedroom.

Apart from the stigmata, the Easter stories offer no indication of Jesus' physical appearance or of the clothes he wore. We are told that his grave clothes had been placed neatly in the tomb and naturally assume that he appeared dressed as did other Galileans at that time, but we know nothing about the texture, colour and quality of his clothes, or if they appeared to be well-worn or new. In contrast, recent reports tend to give more detailed descriptions of his attire and appearance. This difference is not a matter of much importance but it is a point of interest. More significant perhaps is the tactile relationships that have been recorded. We know that the women clasped Jesus' feet in Gethsemane and that he invited Thomas to touch him, and that no other such incidents are recorded in the Gospels. But we also know that similar incidents occur nowadays, both as encounters with Jesus (see Ernie Hollands, Chapter 6) and, from a different perspective, in the reports of bereaved spouses.

## Knowing the risen Jesus

Christians believe in one God, the creator of the universe and source of all life. This one God is regarded as a Trinity: three mutually indwelling and interpenetrating centres of being that are referred to as the Father, the Son and the Holy Spirit. It is clear from their replies that the bishops are very mindful of this special relationship within the Godhead and they are also aware of the problems that can arise if one tries to distinguish between the work of the Holy Spirit and the presence of Jesus the Son. Whilst recognizing this potential for uncertainty and the sustaining power of the Holy Spirit, most bishops (66.6%) report having a relationship with Jesus that is distinct from the relationship they have with the Holy Spirit.

So what does a bishop mean when he says that 'we pray in the Spirit through the Son to the Father'? Probably that the source of our prayer is provided by the Spirit and that, through our relationship with the Son, we direct it to the Father, the source of all creation. One bishop attempted to explain his relationship with the Holy Spirit in this way: 'I can't say that I am consciously expecting the Holy Spirit will help or point the way in discernible signs but I do believe that His sustaining and guiding care is surely and constantly around me, moving and guiding in the whole breadth and depth of my life and circumstances. Then from time to time there is the surprise of a sure sense that things have come together with the sure signs of His mark upon them.'

## Perceiving Jesus

It seems from the bishops' letters that their sense of the presence of God occurs most intensely when they are 'with His people at worship'. Many bishops wrote of such moments and of experiencing a strong spiritual awareness of Christ's presence. This happens often during the Eucharist but also at quite unexpected moments, and occasionally in the shape of another person. Some said the experience was strongest at moments of crisis, perhaps at a deathbed when, to quote another bishop, there might be a 'deep consciousness of the Risen Christ coming to take his child home'. Most bishops had no 'visionary' experiences of Jesus but some were aware of a voice that had called them to his service and one wrote of a significant occasion when the 'room seemed blazing with light'. Another wrote of an occasion in his teens when he had a visionary experience of Jesus as a figure of light, a perception that changed the direction of his life irrevocably. Five bishops said that they had met Jesus in a way comparable to the reports provided in the Acts and Gospels. Four wrote of their experiences briefly, whilst the bishop who provided the fullest account did so 'in strictest confidence' – thus ensuring that his letter could not be published.

The bishops' replies to the questionnaire, their accompanying remarks and letters carry a special authority, but the information provided by other people is also illuminating. A lady I was asked to visit saw Jesus immediately before she died, and similar experiences are recorded elsewhere in this book. In such instances, it is difficult to see any validity in the contention that her experience was just the 'wish fulfilment' perception of a dying person. From a different perspective, Donald English was certain he saw Jesus enter the bedroom of his sick wife and stand close by for a few minutes. It effected him so deeply he was unable to talk about it for a long time. When he felt able to speak of it later, he chose to share the experience with theological students, possibly because he realized that it was important they should be aware of such occurrences.

## Testing the experiences

For the individual the reality of such an unusual personal experience is rarely in doubt; its significance is something each person assesses for themselves. The validity of such experiences for society in general requires more careful elucidation, and this can be undertaken in three ways: by considering its relationship to the teaching of the Church; through the insights provided by neuro-science and psychological practice; and by the application of common sense.

In mainstream denominations the leadership is often wary of reports of mystic visions, tending to dismiss them as subjective fantasies or evidence of a disturbed mind. But when in doubt, they do subject the perceiver's claim to careful scrutiny. Within the Roman Catholic Church, this response is most evident in its handling of Marian visions. For instance, the initial reluctance of the Catholic hierarchy to accept as genuine the reported appearances of the Virgin Mary at Lourdes and Fatima, and its subsequent acceptance of the reality of the visions, provide good examples of the way scepticism is sometimes replaced by official recognition. Sightings of the Blessed Virgin appear to be relatively common and, according to data given at a seminar on Marian studies in 1986, an estimated 21,000 sightings of the Virgin Mary have been reported during the past 1,000 years. [2] This figure is much higher than for sightings of Jesus.

There is always uncertainty about the authenticity of such visions. Each has to be assessed on its own merits. One unusual instance was recounted to a congregation, of which I was a member, by an Anglican priest who accepted that it was not a veridical experience. He told us that he was standing alone in a country church, gazing at an altar that had a frontal with an embroidered figure of Jesus. Then he saw the figure of Jesus move. It seemed to dance and rotate and it spoke to him, though the words he heard were totally incomprehensible. The voice was not an inner voice but came directly from the figure on the frontal. The experience was not uplifting; there was something disturbing about it and the priest very sensibly sought advice from people he trusted. He consulted them separately but they all offered the same general advice. This was to accept the incident as a significant experience, not to overrate its importance and to keep his feet firmly on the ground. That advice might easily have been given by St John of the Cross.

## St John of the Cross

Encounters with Jesus have been recorded over many centuries. During the Middle Ages, St John of the Cross and his friend St Theresa of Avila had many mystical–psychical experiences to draw upon when advising others. St John recorded some of his mystical experiences most beautifully in his poetry – his commentaries on these works tending to emphasize the importance of an ascetic lifestyle and purification of the soul by divine grace. When asked about visions he wrote: 'We should close our eyes to these psychic phenomena and reject them whatever their source. Otherwise we are preparing the way for those that come from the devil and giving Satan such influence that not only will his visions take the place of God's, but, while his increase, those of God will decrease.' [3]

Elsewhere, he again stresses the importance of faith and the danger of visions whatever their source. He considered visions undesirable even if they came from God, and his reasons for saying so are as follows:

1. Faith gradually diminishes because what is experienced by

the senses detracts from faith... and so the soul... withdraws from means of union with God.

2. Things of the senses, if they are not rejected, are an obstacle to the spirit.

3. The soul becomes dependent upon these phenomena and does not advance to true contentment and detachment.

4. The soul begins to lose the favours granted by God, because it feeds upon these as though by right. But God, in giving them, does not intend that the soul should seek after them or rest in them. Indeed it should not be presumed that such phenomena come from God. [4]

## St Theresa of Avila

St Theresa of Avila and St John of the Cross were Discalced (reformed) Carmelites, St Theresa having established the first reformed house in 1562 with thirteen nuns who had elected to join her in conditions of poverty, solitude and hardship. Their lifestyle was simple and the diet vegetarian. Both saints were declared a Doctor of the Church (St John in 1926 and St Theresa in 1970), Theresa being the first woman to be so honoured. She wrote authoritatively about apparitions, visions and union with God, and her letters included advice on the ways to distinguish between communications and visions sent by the devil and those that came from God. She seems to have experienced both. In one vision an angel thrust a golden spear tipped with burning iron into Theresa's heart and did so with such force that it pierced the saint's intestines. Of another vision she wrote: 'Once whilst I was reciting with all the Sisters the hours of the Divine Office, my soul suddenly became recollected; and it seemed to me to be like a brightly polished mirror, without any part on the back or sides or top or bottom that wasn't totally clear. In its centre Christ, our Lord, was shown to me... I was given understanding of what it is for a soul to be in mortal sin. It amounts to clouding this mirror with mist and leaving it black; and thus this Lord cannot be revealed or seen even though He is always present giving us being.' [5]

The frequency and nature of Theresa's visions and consolations are remarkable yet she, and St John of the Cross, were careful not to rate them over highly. Various explanations can be offered for the visions they had at that time. Their limited diet may have included hallucinogenic mushrooms from the surrounding hills, and their strict monastic routine, with its long hours of silent prayer and contemplation, may have produced sensory deprivation, itself a well-known cause of hallucinatory experiences. Hallucinations can be induced by isolation, hunger and physical hardship, conditions which St John of the Cross experienced during his imprisonment by brother monks at Toledo, where he was starved, physically ill-treated and accused of heresy. Eventually, he was forced to make a perilous escape in order to survive – an escape which later featured in one of his poems.

St Theresa seems to have been less dismissive of mystical experiences than was St John of the Cross. She drew an important distinction between visions of Christ that were of the intellect and those of the imagination. Of the former she said, 'Whilst the soul is heedless of any (such) thought…it will feel Jesus Christ our Lord, beside it. Yet it does not see Him, either with the eyes of the body or those of the soul.' This she called an 'intellectual vision'. [6] Of imaginative visions she wrote: 'When our Lord is pleased to give more delight to this soul, He shows it clearly His most sacred humanity in the way He desires; either as He was when He went about in the world or as He is after His Resurrection. And even though the vision happens so quickly that we could compare it to a streak of lightning, this most glorious image remains so engraved on the imagination that I think it would be impossible to erase it.' To this comment she added, 'Though I say image, let it be understood that...it is not a painting but truly alive.' [7]

There was one experience that Theresa considered surpassed both the intellectual and the imaginative visions. This she called the spiritual marriage. Of it she wrote: 'The Lord appears in the centre of the soul, not in an imaginative vision but in an intellectual one, although more delicate than those mentioned, as He appeared to the apostles when entering through the door when he said to them *pax vobis*. Then the delight the soul experiences is so extreme – that I do not know what to compare it to. I can say only that the Lord wishes to reveal for that moment...the glory of heaven. One can say no more than that the soul, I mean the spirit, is made one with God.' [8]

Similar distinctions were made much earlier. St Augustine of Hippo (354-430), for instance, classified visions as corporeal, imaginative and intellectual, [9] whilst Julian of Norwich said of the revelations that were granted to her that they came by physical sight, by words formed in my intellect and by spiritual sight. Of spiritual sight, she said, 'I can never describe it fully,' and, 'It is the will of God that of all the qualities of the blessed Trinity that we should be most sure of, and delighted with, is love. Love makes might and wisdom come down to our level.' [10] St Theresa of Avila would certainly agree with that assessment. Whilst Theresa had many visionary and ecstatic moments, she knew that the purpose of these spiritual gifts was not 'solely to give delight to souls', but 'are meant to fortify our weaknesses' so that we can serve others, particularly those close to us. She concluded with this advice to her Sisters in the convent: 'We shouldn't build castles in the air. The Lord does not look at the greatness of our works but the love with which they are done.' [11]

## Resurrection and Al Isra

The nature of Christ's Resurrection body has been discussed briefly already. The uncertainty surrounding it – whether it was a physical or spiritual body, or a body composed of non-carbon elements, remains a matter of conjecture and/or faith. A modern sceptic can rightly say that 'we have no way of knowing with certainty the truth of the matter'. However, it is not just a Christian problem; similar uncertainties exist in the Muslim world. The *Holy Qu'ran* says of Jesus that 'Allah raised him up unto Himself'. Varying interpretations are given to this verse but the one that is generally accepted by Muslims is that Jesus did not die the usual human death but lives in the body in heaven. [12] A similar uncertainty exists regarding the *Al Isra* (Night journey), one of the most significant episodes in the life of the Prophet Muhammad.

The *Al Isra* is a title given to Surah 17 of the *Qur'an*. In the opening verse we are told that 'Allah did take his Servant for a journey by night' and that during the journey the Prophet was transported from the Sacred Mosque (of Maccah) to the Farthest Mosque (of Jerusalem). The mosques were blessed and, according to the Hadith literature, Muhammad ascended through the seven heavens to the Sublime Throne. There he met and talked with the Prophets who had preceded him, was granted an ineffable vision of Allah, and initiated into the spiritual mysteries of the human soul's struggle throughout eternity. The majority of commentators take this night journey literally and accept that, for the journey, the Prophet's body was transformed into spiritual fineness. [13]

More details of this journey are recorded in the Hadith literature. This is a record of the Prophet's sayings and actions which his Companions collected after Muhammad's death and are considered to be genuine. It has become the basis of the developed law, theology and custom that is Islam, and is of

220

immense importance in the everyday life of Muslim men and women. [14] Hadith provides the believer with an intimate knowledge of Muhammad's life and offers each one the 'perfect exemplar' of the Muslim way, enabling them to feel close to the Prophet, 'loving him not only as master and guide but also as brother-man'. The similarity with the Christian attitude to Jesus is close, though Islam would never condone the deification of the Prophet. More specifically, the record of the 'night journey' provides Muslims with uncertainties about the nature of the Prophet's body during the journey, uncertainties that Christians may associate with Jesus' body at the Resurrection and Ascension. In both instances, resolution of the problem is determined by faith in its corporeal reality, or a metaphorical interpretation of the bodily nature of the event, or a not yet elucidated scientific explanation.

## Conclusion

A bishop posed the question that needs to be answered now, when he asked, 'Is there any difference between the post-Resurrection appearances of Christ (i.e. those that occurred before the Ascension) and the ones that individuals say they see today?' When I read that question for the first time, in 2004, my immediate response was: 'I do not know the answer.' Now, having collected and considered the evidence, my position is less uncertain. It is apparent that there are many similarities between Christ's Resurrection appearances and those that have been reported since his Ascension. There are important differences too, and these need to be discussed. But before considering them, the following comment written by Peter Cooke after he had read a draft of the manuscript may be illuminating. He wrote:

> 'I have real problems with the section, "Meeting the Risen Jesus; then and now." The main problem, from the view of Biblical

Scholarship, is that it relies so heavily on narrative details from the Gospels (and Acts) for a comparison with contemporary encounters. You have not taken into account the compressing, formularising and 'narrativization' processes which may well have gone into producing the stories we have. Indescribable, transcendental experiences had to be shaped for preaching purposes, and later for reading purposes, into comprehensible and memorable chunks. Therefore the details you rely on may well be 'narrative inventions' intended to express the transcendental truths about the '40 days' to a post-apostolic audience of converts, or potential converts. Typically, the details are emphasized in such a way as to highlight the mystery and ambiguity of the resurrected Jesus. To talk about his appearing as an 'ordinary human person', and of his clothes etc, seems to me to bring the stories too much 'down to earth' for the purpose of supporting your analogies, whereas the stories are attempting to catch the inexpressible for a largely unsophisticated audience.' [15]

Peter Cooke's *caveat* is a useful reminder that a literal interpretation of the Gospel stories is not always appropriate, but it is the only evidence we have with which to compare Christ's more recent appearances with those of the Resurrection. The following variants are noteworthy. At the Resurrection:

1. His closest followers failed to recognize him.

2. They were frightened of him

3. Some thought he was a ghost

4. Their lives were not changed immediately.

5. Apart from improving the catch of the fishermen (John 21: 3-6), his presence brought no apparent immediate gain, spiritually or materially.

These differences are important, and if they had not been applied to the Resurrection appearances but to present-day experiences of Christ, they might be used to belittle the reality of the more recent encounters. But belief in an afterlife and that Christ is Risen, is reinforced by contemporary accounts of meetings with the risen Jesus. Like the Gospel narratives, they have universal importance and help to remind us that Christ is not restricted by time or place, and that we should not restrict our understanding of the Resurrection and afterlife to the insights of the early Church Fathers. As Paul reminded us, they too 'only see through a glass darkly' (1 Corinthians 13: 12). This is not to say that the disciples' meetings with Jesus and those of people today are of equal significance, but some do carry close similarities. In other words they are analogous, different but similar, and this also applies to bereavement experiences. Both point to the Resurrection of the dead, first in Christ and then for the rest of humanity.

Regarding the Christic visions, Professor Wiebe takes a firmer stance than I do. He says, 'I do not think the evidence supports the position that the NT appearance accounts are *very* different from post-biblical apparition accounts.' [16] Later, he says: 'The contention that the probability of the Resurrection is high, and cannot be significantly enhanced by evidence additional to that coming from the NT appearance stories, is suspect.' [17] He supports this conclusion with a statistical assessment of his data using a probability argument, which I am told by a statistician does not support his argument, as it is possible to reach the exact opposite of Wiebe's conclusion from the information given. However, I think that Wiebe's conclusions are justified anyway and do not need the support of statistical tests.

There is a striking similarity between the perceptions of widowed people when they speak of their dead spouse and St Theresa's description of the different types of visions that she had of Jesus. Of the intellectual vision, she wrote that the perceiver 'feel(s) Jesus Christ our Lord beside it. Yet it does not see Him, either with the eyes of the body or those of the soul'. [6] This sense of Jesus being beside her is similar to the 'sense of the deceased's presence' reported by widowed people. Of the imaginative visions, Theresa said that 'He shows it clearly His most sacred humanity in the way He desires; either as He was when He went about in the world or as He is after His Resurrection'. [7] Again this is evocative of the data provided by widowed people who say that they have seen their deceased spouse in normal everyday situations.

Finally, people of many different beliefs perceive the presence of their dead partners when widowed. It is a universal finding that crosses cultural and religious boundaries, and is possibly the main reason for the widely-held belief that life continues after death. I wonder if theologians from different religious traditions have ever discussed together their attitudes to this belief. It could be a contentious issue. On the other hand, if they look at the available evidence, they may find much on which they could agree.

# Appendices

## Appendix 1

Notice in Coventry Cathedral newsletter

The following notice was included in a leaflet given to members of the congregation attending the ordination service at Coventry Cathedral on Sunday, 4 July 2004.

Meeting Jesus

People sometimes speak of having had a personal encounter/ experience of the Risen Christ. I am never quite sure what this means or how frequently such experiences occur or who is most likely to have them, and would very much like to explore this aspect of Christian life with members of the congregation. If anyone is willing to share what must be a very significant and personal experience with me, I would very much like to meet them. I can be contacted in the cathedral after the Sunday Eucharist – I am the elderly man with white hair, glasses and a wife called Valerie – or by telephone (given) or on e-mail (given). David Rees.

## Appendix 2

Letter to Coventry Diocesan Cursillistas

Dear Friend

Meeting the Risen Jesus

In his book on the Resurrection (*Easter Faith*) the Catholic theologian Fr Gerald O'Collins refers to a paper I published in 1971. He speaks kindly of my work but interprets its significance in a way that I would not do now. I think the best way for me to deal with the issues that arise is to provide a brief commentary on the Resurrection from the viewpoint of a medical layman. It would help me to formulate a reply if I could obtain a clearer understanding of the frequency with which people have an encounter with the risen Jesus. This is not so unusual as it may seem and among the reports I have collected is one by the Revd Dr Donald English (twice President of the Methodist Conference) who describes seeing Jesus in the room where his wife was receiving healing for terminal cancer. He said that Jesus appeared as a solid figure who remained in the room for 3-4 minutes and then walked out through the door.

I realize that as individuals our relationship with Jesus and the Holy Spirit covers a wide range of experiences and whilst looking primarily for Road to Emmaus type of occurrences I would very much like to meet any member of Cursillo who has had a significant encounter with Jesus that they may be willing to share with me. I can be contacted by post, telephone, e-mail or at an Ultreya. I am willing to travel.

## Appendix 3

Letter to retired bishops:

21 July 2004

The Hon. Assistant Bishop in…

Dear Bishop,

Meeting Jesus like the Apostles did?

I wish to write a book on the Resurrection. The idea has been in my thoughts for some years but became more focussed a few weeks ago after I had purchased a copy of *Easter Faith* by the Catholic theologian, Fr Gerald O'Collins. I had read a review of the book in *The Tablet* and ordered it from the journal's bookshop receiving it by post. As I glanced through the book I was surprised to find that two pages in the opening chapter dealt almost exclusively with a paper that I had published in the *British Medical Journal*, in 1971, on bereavement.

Fr O'Collins speaks kindly of my work but interprets its significance in a way that I do not consider appropriate now. He mentions also a book by Professor Phillip Weibe, the Dean of Arts and Religious

Studies at Trinity Western University, Canada, entitled *Visions of Jesus*. Professor Weibe's approach to the subject differs from that of Fr O'Collins by, *inter alia*, including statements from people who say they have seen Jesus in recent years. In some ways this is groundbreaking work but as Professor Weibe points out there is a 'paucity' of information on the subject and much needs to be done to clarify the situation. I believe that much more could also be done by non-theological disciplines to make the Resurrection meaningful to the modern mind. These include my own profession of medicine and it is to be regretted that the close relationship that once existed between the Church and medicine no longer exists. The days for instance when the Archbishop of Canterbury was a qualified medical doctor are long past. Archbishop Secker who took his medical degree in Leyden in 1721 being the last physician to hold that ecclesiastical post.

I know a number of instances where Christians believe they have seen Jesus in the way listed by Paul in 1 Corinthians 15: 3-8. Among these is the Road to Emmaus type of experience recorded by Kenneth McAll in *Healing the Family Tree*, and the incident reported by Donald English, a Methodist minister who was, unusually, twice elected President of the Methodist Conference. Dr English was naturally reluctant to speak of his experiences but did mention it to a few people including Jeff Jefferies, who was present when the incident occurred and who I visited yesterday. It happened when Jeff was giving healing to Bertha English, then terminally ill with cancer, and took place in the house in the Cotswolds where Dr and Mrs English were staying. Jeff had just finished the prayer for healing when Donald, who was sitting on the opposite side of the bed looked up and saw Jesus standing a short distance behind Jeff. He said that the figure was clearly discernible, solid — not ghostly or transparent, and remained in the room for 3-4 minutes before walking out through the door. There is, of course, no firm evidence or certainty that it was Jesus but that is the interpretation Donald English gave to what he perceived.

Bishop Cuthbert Bardsley also claimed to have seen Christ in an objective physical manner. Archbishop Coggan does not mention the incident in his biography of Cuthbert Bardsley but Bp Bardsley writes of it in his foreword to Kathleen Browning's book *See Through* and this is quoted in J Ernst's book *Dorothy Kerin*. The incident took place in All Saints Church, Leamington Spa, where Dorothy Kerin was conducting a healing service a few months before she died. She looked so frail as she mounted the pulpit that Cuthbert prayed for Jesus to be there supporting her. 'Then,' he said, 'a remarkable thing happened. Over Dorothy's face gradually appeared the face of Christ, until it was quite clear. For a few minutes the beloved face of Our Lord was there, and then gradually faded away, and Dorothy's face had returned. I had clearly been shown that Christ was already there to strengthen her, and she carried on bravely to the end of the service.'

Whilst experiences of this type are very personal, they are also of importance to the wider community and need to be more generally known. The frequency with which they occur also needs to be more clearly determined. It is for this reason that I am seeking data from three groups of people who are associated with the Church of England, some perhaps just nominally, others by a lifetime of service and commitment. The people being approached are:

Firstly those who attended the ordination service at Coventry Cathedral on Sunday 4 July 2004 – I have received some interesting responses.

Secondly members of the Coventry Diocesan Cursillo – I am myself a cursillista.

Thirdly the Honorary Assistant Bishops in the Church of England. Of those listed in Crockford's, seven reside overseas and 14 are aged over 85 so I am writing only to those who live in England and were born after 1920. Bishops are a very special group of Christians, and I hope that you will have the time and inclination to think about and respond to the contents of this letter. I know that some of you have had experiences similar to those mentioned above.

I am asking you to do two things. The first is to complete the questionnaire given overleaf and return it to me in the enclosed stamped, addressed envelope. Secondly and more importantly, I would be most interested to hear your views about the Resurrection, and also of any personal experiences of Jesus – subjective or otherwise, that you may care to share with me and perhaps a wider audience if my book gets written and published.

Thank you for your patience in reading this letter.

It comes with my best wishes.

Yours sincerely

## Appendix 4

Questionnaire

1. We know that 'we live and move and have our being in Him'. Apart from this do you feel that the Holy Spirit is helping and guiding you in a discernible way?

$$\text{Yes [ ]} \qquad \text{No [ ]}$$

2. We meet Jesus in a special way in the Sacraments. Apart from this, do you ever feel that Jesus as distinct from the Holy Spirit is with you, perhaps in a way that is difficult to describe in words?

$$\text{Yes [ ]} \qquad \text{No [ ]}$$

3. Have you ever had a clear, perception of the risen Jesus, similar to that listed by Paul in 1 Corinthians 15: 3-8 and recorded in the Gospels?

$$\text{Yes [ ]} \qquad \text{No [ ]}$$

The answers given to this questionnaire will be regarded as strictly confidential and used only for statistical purposes.

# REFERENCES

**Chapter 1. Personal Foreword**

1    Evans E (1987) *The Welsh Revival of 1904* (Third Edition) Bridgend. Bryntitrion Press pp 146–160.

2    Hocken P (1997) *Streams of Renewal* Carlisle. Paternoster Press p 1.

3    Evans E (1987) *The Welsh Revival of 1904* (Third Edition) Bridgend. Bryntirion Press pp 192–3.

4    Gibbard N (2005) *Fire on the Altar* Bridgend. Bryntirion Press p 200.

5    Rees WD, Lutkins SG (1967) 'Mortality of Bereavement.' *British Medical Journal* 4: 13–16.

6    Rees WD (1971) 'The Hallucinations of Widowhood.' *British Medical Journal* 4: 37–41.

7    Sloan RP, Bagiella E, Powell T (1999) 'Religion, Spirituality, and Medicine.' *The Lancet* 353: 664–7.


**Chapter 2. Jesus Crucified**

1    Josephus Flavius (0063) *Antiquities of the Jews*. Book 18, Ch 3, paragraph 3. Translated by William Whiston (1732). Project Gutenberg Etext.

2    Tacitus (0116) Annals. Loeb editions 15, 44. Cited on web by Mark Eastman in *Blue Letter Bible Commentaries*: Appendix 2, Historical Evidence for Jesus.

3    Bucklin, R (1970) 'The legal and medical aspects of the trial and death of Christ.' *Science and Law* 10: 14–26.

4    Lloyd Davies M and Lloyd Davies T A (1991) 'Resurrection or Resuscitation.' *Journal of the Royal College of the Physicians of London* 25: No. 2 pp 167–70.

5    Brenner, Benjamin (2005) Quoted in 'Faith News', *The Times*, Saturday, June 11, p 76 and by Minerva in British Medical Journal (2005) Volume 330, p 1,456.

6    Murphy-O'Connor, Jerome (2005) 'Christ's Final Journey.' *The Tablet*, March 26, pp 6–7.

7    Josephus, Flavius (0099) *Life of Flavius Josephus* para 75. Translated by William Whiston (1732). Project Gutenberg Etext.

8    *The Holy Qur'an*. Text, Translation and Commentary by Abdullah Yusuf Ali. New Revised Edition (1989). Brentwood. Maryland, Amana Corporation, pp 235–6.

### Chapter 3. Resurrection

1  Ginsberg, Louis (1964) Quoted by Rabbi H Rabonowicz in *A Guide to Life. Jewish Laws and Customs of Mourning*. London Jewish Chronicle Publications, p 132.

### Chapter 4. Contacting the Bishops

1  Rees W D (1971) 'The Hallucinations of Widowhood.' *British Medical Journal* 4: 37–41.

2  O'Collins, Gerald (2003) *Easter Faith: Believing in the Risen Jesus*. London. Darton, Longman and Todd. p 13.

3  Wiebe, Phillip H (1997) *Visions of Jesus*. New York and Oxford. Oxford University Press. pp 41–2.

4  *Crockfords Directory of Anglican Clergy* (2003).

5  Wiebe, Phillip (1997) Oxford University Press. p 225.

6  Osis K, Haraldsson E (1977) 'Deathbed observations by physicians and nurses: a cross-cultural survey.' *The Journal of the American Society for Psychical Research* 71: 238–59.

7  Bardsley, C (1974) Foreword to Kathleen Browning, *See Through*. Quoted in J Ernest's (1987) *Dorothy Kerin*. Oxford. University Printing House. pp 74–5.

### Chapter 5. Bishops' Replies.

1  Loyola, Ignatius (1491–1556) *The Spiritual Exercises*, translated by Thomas Corbishley. Wheathampstead. Anthony Clarke p 9.

2  Maddocks, Morris (1990) *The Christian Healing Ministry*. London. SPCK.

### Chapter 6. Meeting Jesus.

1  Julian of Norwich (1373) *Revelations of Divine Love*. Translated by Clifton Wolters (1966). Harmondsworth. Penguin Classics. pp 191–2.

2  Montefiore, Hugh (1995) *Oh God, What Next?* London. Hodder and Stoughton. p 1.

3  Montefiore, Hugh (1995) *ibid*. p 2.

4  Cooke, Peter (2005) personal communication.

5  MacCaffery J (1978) *The Friar of Giovanni. Tales of Padre Pio*. London. Darton, Longman and Todd.

6  Maddocks, Morris (1999) *The Vision of Dorothy Kerin*. Guildford. Eagle. p 88.

7  St Theresa of Avila (1515–82) *The Collected Works of St Theresa of Avila, Volume 2*. Translated by Kieran Kavanagh and Otilio Rodriguez (1980). Washington DC. ICS Publications pp 405–10.

8    St Theresa of Avila (1515–82) *ibid.* p 411.

9    St Theresa of Avila (1515–82) *ibid.* p 433–4.

10   Wiebe Phillip H (1997) *Visions of Christ.* Oxford. Oxford University Press. pp 72–4.

11   Wiebe Phillip H (1997) *ibid.* p 227.

12   Wiebe Phillip H (1997) *ibid.* pp 52–3.

13   Minter Ken (c1991) In Part 1 of the videotape recording entitled 'The Ministry of Christian Healing'. issued by the Pin Mill Christian Healing Fellowship. Felixstowe, Suffolk.

14   Dillistone FW (1975) *Charles Raven.* London. Hodder and Stoughton. p 63.

15   Cooke, Peter (2005) personal communication

**Chapter 7. Deathbed Experiences.**

1    Maddox, Morris (1990) *The Christian Healing Ministry.* London. SPCK. pp 118–9.

2    Montefiori, Hugh (1995) *Oh God, What Next?* London. Hodder and Stoughton p 18.

3    Robinson, Edward (1978) *Living the Questions.* Oxford. The Religious Experience Research Unit, Manchester College pp 137–9.

4    Osis K, Haraldsson E (1977) 'Deathbed observations by physicians and nurses: a cross-cultural survey.' *The Journal of the American Society for Psychical Research* 71: 238–59.

5    Rogo, D Scott (1989) *The Return from Silence.* Wellingborough. Aquarian Press.

6    Grey, Margot (1985) *Return from Death.* London. Arkana.

7    Moody, R and Perry, P (1989) *The Light Beyond.* London. Pan Books. pp vii–viii.

8    Sogyal Rinpoche (1992) *The Tibetan Book of Living and Dying.* London. Rider. pp 217–8.

9    Freud, Sigmund (1957) *Thoughts for the Times on Death and War. Volume 14 of the Standard Edition of the Complete Psychological Works of Sigmund Freud.* Toronto. Hogarth. pp 292–6.

10   Barrett, Sir William (1926) *Deathbed Visions.* Wellingborough: The Aquarian Press. p 57.

11   Kerin, Dorothy (1952) *Fulfilling.* Tunbridge Wells. K&SC Printers Ltd. p 80.

12   von Franz, Marie-Louise (1987) *On Dreams and Death.* London. Shambhala. pp 41–55.

13   Jefferies, Esmond (1999) 'The Vision of the Risen Christ.' In *Life-Line,* Issue No 31, a publication of the Pin Mill Christian Healing Fellowship. Felixstowe, Suffolk. pp 2–5.

14    English, Donald (1998) 'The Experience of Healing.' In *Life-Line*, Issue No 31, a publication of the Pin Mill Christian Healing Fellowship. Felixstowe, Suffolk. pp 3–4.

15    Jefferies, Esmond (1999) *ibid.*

16    English, Donald (1998) 'The Experience of Healing.' In *Life-Line*, Issue No 31, A publication of the Pin Mill Christian Healing Fellowship. Felixstowe, Suffolk. p 6.

17    Murray, Iain H (1982) *D. Martyn Lloyd-Jones. The First Forty Years 1899–1939.* Edinburgh. The Banner of Truth Press. p 247.

18    Rees, W Dewi (1972) 'The Distress of Dying.' *British Medical Journal* 3: 105–107.


## Chapter 8. A Healing Ministry

1    McAll, Kenneth (1986) *Healing The Family Tree.* (New Edition) London. Sheldon Press. pp 1–2.

2    McAll, Frances and Kenneth (1987) *The Moon Looking Down.* London. Darley Anderson. pp 87–8.

3    McAll, Kenneth (1996) 'Healing Through The Eucharist Part 1.' *The Family Tree Ministry Journal*: No 4. p 17.

4    McAll, Kenneth (1996) 'Healing Through The Eucharist Part 1.' *The Family Tree Ministry Journal*: No 4. p 17.

5    McAll, Frances (1996) *The Family Tree Ministry Journal*: No 4. p 3.

6    Hughes, Gerard, W (2003) *God in All Things.* London. Hodder and Stoughton. p 208.

7    Baker, Hugh D R (1979) *Chinese Family and Kinship.* London. The MacMillan Press. p 72.

8    Wells, David (2003) *Praying for the Family Tree.* The Generational Healing Trust. www.healingtrust.info

9    Cooke, Peter (2006) Personal communication


## Chapter 9. Other Cultures

1    Lemon, Fred with Gladys Knowlton (1977) *Breakout.* London. Lakeland. p 109.

2    Roberts George, E (1977) Foreword to *Breakout* by Fred Lemon with Gladys Knowlton. London. Lakeland.

3    *Celebrating Common Prayer: The Pocket Version* (1994) London. Mowbray. p 16.

4    Backhouse, Halcyon (1985) editor and Introduction. *At the Feet of the Master* by Sadhu Sundar Singh, translated from the Urdu by the Revd Arthur and Mrs Parker (1922). London. Hodder and Stoughton. pp 15–16.

5    Weibe, Phillip (1997) *Visions of Jesus.* Oxford University Press. pp 52–3.

## Chapter 10. Widows' Tales

1     Rogo, D Scott (1986) *Case for Survival of Bodily Death*. The Aquarian Press. p 81.

2     Rees, W D (1971) *The Hallucinatory Reactions of Bereavement*. MD thesis. University of London Library. The Senate House. Russell Square. London.

3     Rees, W D (1971) 'The hallucinations of widowhood.' *British Medical Journal* 4: 37–41.

4     Rees, Dewi (2001) *Death and Bereavement: The psychological, religious and cultural interfaces*. London. Whurr Publishers pp 256–281.

5     Haraldsson, E (1988) 'Survey of claimed encounters with the dead.' *Omega* 19(2): 103–113.

6     Greeley, A M (1975) *The Sociology of the Paranormal: A Reconnaissance*. Beverley Hills. Sage Publications. p 29.

7     Glick I O, Weiss R S, Parkes C M (1974) *The First Year of Bereavement*. New York. John Wiley/Interscience.

8     Silverman P R, Worden J W (1993) 'Children's reactions to the death of a parent.' In Stroebe MS, Stroebe W, Hansson R O (eds) *Handbook of Bereavement: Theory, Research and Intervention*. Cambridge University Press. p 309.

9     Olson P R et al (1985) 'Hallucinations of widowhood.' *Journal of the American Geriatric Society* 33: 543–7.

10    Christian Deliverance Study Group (1996) *Deliverance. Psychic Deliverance and Occult Involvement*. Michael Perry (editor) London: SPCK.

11    Robert F John (2002) 'Mrs Hatton, the Maori, my Dad, me and the Resurrection.' *The Expository Times*: Vol. 113, No.7, pp 226–9.

12    Roberts F John (2005) personal communication

## Chapter 11. Are the Experiences Comparable?

1     O'Collins, Gerard (2003) *Easter Faith: Believing in the Risen Jesus*. London. Darton, Longman and Todd. pp 12–13.

2     Rees, Dewi (2001) *Death and Bereavement: The psychological, religious and cultural interfaces*. (Second edition). London/Philadelphia, Whurr Publishers. pp 276–80.

3     Ward, Keith (2005) 'The Quantum leap.' *The Tablet* (2 April 2005) p 9.

4     Lewis, C S (1961) *A Grief Observed*. London. Faber.

5     Peters T, Russell R J, Welker M (2002) *Resurrection: Theological and Scientific Assessments*. Grand Rapids/Cambridge. Wm. B Eerdmans.

6     Wright N T (2003) *The Resurrection of the Son of God*. London. SPCK. p 690.

7     Roberts F J (2002) 'Mrs Hatton, the Maori, Fred, me and the Resurrection.' *The Expository Times*. pp 226–9.

8     Montefiore, Hugh (2002) *The Paranormal: A Bishop Investigates.* Leicestershire. Upfront Publishing, p 219.

## Chapter 12. Intimations of Immortality

1     Ward Keith (2005) 'The Quantum leap.' *The Tablet* (2 April 2005) p 9.

2     Ashton, Joan (1988) *Mother of Nations: Visions of Mary.* Basingstoke. The Lamp Press p 188.

3     St John of the Cross (1542–91) 'The Ascent of Mount Carmel.' In Elizabeth Hamilton (Editor and translator) *The Voice of the Spirit: The Spirituality of St John of the Cross.* (1976). London. Darton, Longmann and Todd, p 45.

4     St John of the Cross (1542–91) *ibid.* p 48.

5     St Theresa of Avila (1515–82) *The Collected Works of St Theresa of Avila, Volume 2.* Translated by Kieran Kavanagh and Otilio Rodriguez (1980). Washington DC. ICS Publications p 269.

6     St Theresa of Avila (1515–82) *ibid.* p 405.

7     St Theresa of Avila (1515–82) *ibid.* p 411.

8     St Theresa of Avila (1515–82) *ibid.* pp 433–4.

9     Wiebe, Phillip (1997) *Visions of Jesus.* Oxford University Press. p 21.

10    Julian of Norwich (1342–1416) *Revelations of Divine Love.* Translated by Clifton Wolters. (1966) Harmondsworth. Penguin Books, p 191–3.

11    St Theresa of Avila (1515–82) *ibid.* pp 445 and 450.

12    *The Holy Qur'an* Text, Translation and Commentary by Abdullah Yusuf Ali. New Revised Edition (1989) Brentwood Maryland, Amana Corporation, Surah 3: 55-58. pp 141–2.

13    *Ibid.* pp 671–3.

14    Chapman, Colin (1996) *Cross and Crescent.* Inter-Varsity Press, pp 96–8.

15    Cooke, Peter (2006) personal communication

16    Wiebe, Phillip (1997) *ibid.* p 31.

17    Wiebe, Phillip (1997) *ibid.* p 230.

# BIBLIOGRAPHY

Books mentioned in the text but not included in the references

Alison, James. *The Joy of Being Wrong* (New York, Crossroad, 1998).

Anon (Translated by G Singh), *Sri Guru Granth Sahib* (Delhi, Gus Das Kapur, 1964).

Anon (Translated by Clifton Woltors), *The Cloud of Unknowing* (Harmondsworth, Penguin Classics, 1961).

Anon (Translated by RM French), *The Way of the Pilgrim* (London, SPCK, 1963).

Anon, *Upanishads*.

Anon (Translated by Juan Mascaro), *The Bhagavad Gita* (Harmondsworth, Penguin Classics, 1962).

Browne, Sir Thomas, *Religio Medici* (1643).

Bunyan, John, *The Pilgrim's Progress* (1678).

Cocks, Michael, *The St Stephen Experience* (Auckland, Kelso, 2001).

Kelly, Thomas, R, *A Testament of Devotion* (London, Hodder and Stoughton, 1941).

Lewis, C S, *Miracles* (London, Centenary Press, 1947).

Montefiori, Hugh, *The Paranormal – A Bishop Investigates* (Upfront Publishers; available from Avalon).

Moody, Raymond, *Life after Life* (Atlanta, Mockingbird Books, 1975).

Morrison, Frank, *Who Moved the Stone?* (London, Faber, 1930).

Peters T, Russell R J, Welker M, *Resurrection Theological and Scientific Assessments* (Michigan/Cambridge, Eerdmanns, 2002).

Scott, Christine and Gledhill, Ruth (ed.) *The Times Book of Best Sermons* (London, Cassell, 1998).

Wotton, Henry (1568–1639), 'Upon the Death of Sir Albert Morton's Wife' (poem).

Wright, N T, *The Resurrection of the Son of God* (London, SPCK, 2003).